ENGLISH FRENCH

Dictionary and Word Book

By Colin Clark
Illustrated by Vivienne Bray
and Judy Hensman
Translation by Dominique Cook

ANGLAIS FRANÇAIS

Dictionnaire et Vocabulaire

Brown Watson
ENGLAND

Aa

acrobat / *l'acrobate*

An **acrobat** does jumping and balancing tricks.

*Un **acrobate** fait des sauts et des tours d'équilibre.*

actor / *l'acteur*

An **actor** pretends to be another person in a film or a play.

*Un **acteur** fait semblant d'être une autre personne dans un film ou une pièce de théâtre.*

address / *l'adresse*

The **address** on a letter says where you live.

*L'**adresse** sur une lettre montre où tu habites.*

aircraft / *l'avion*

An **aircraft** is a machine that flies in the sky.

*Un **avion** est une machine qui vole dans le ciel.*

airport / *l'aéroport*

You can see lots of **aircraft** landing and taking off at an **airport**.

*Tu peux voir beaucoup d'avions atterrir et décoller à l'**aéroport**.*

alphabet / *l'alphabet*

All the words that we speak or write are made up of the letters of the **alphabet**.

*Tous les mots que nous disons ou écrivons sont formés avec les lettres de l'**alphabet**.*

ambulance / *l'ambulance*

An **ambulance** takes sick people to hospital.

*Une **ambulance** emmène les gens malades à l'hospital.*

animal / *l'animal*

Any living thing that can move about and feel is called an **animal**.

*Tout être vivant qui peut bouger et ressentir des choses s'appelle un **animal**.*

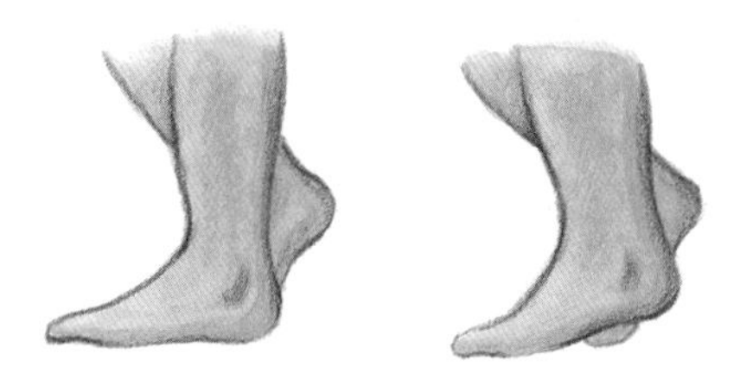

ankle / *la cheville*

The **ankle** joins the leg to the foot.

*La **cheville** relie la jambe au pied*

apple / *la pomme*

An **apple** is a fruit. **Apples** are good to eat.

*La **pomme** est un fruit. Les pommes ont bon goût.*

apron / *le tablier*

When someone is cooking, they wear an **apron** to keep their clothes clean.

*Lorsque quelqu'un cuisine, il porte un **tablier** pour ne pas salir ses vêtements.*

arm / *le bras*

Your **arm** is between your shoulder and your hand.

*Ton **bras** se trouve entre ton épaule et ta main.*

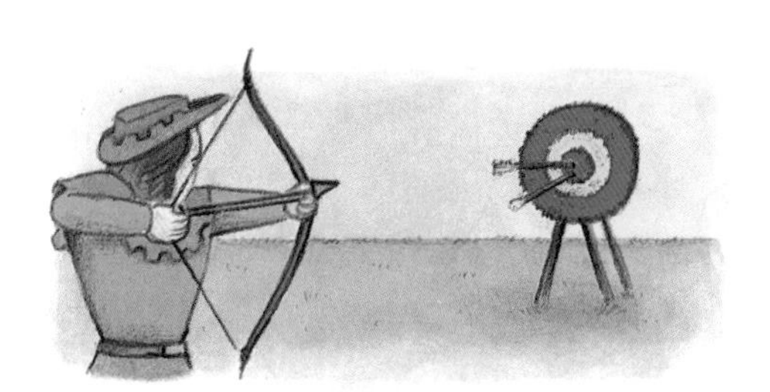

arrow / *la flèche*

An **arrow** is fired through the air from a bow.

*On tire une **flèche** en l'air avec un arc.*

artist / *l'artiste*

The person painting the picture is called an **artist**.

*La personne qui peint le tableau s'appelle un **artiste**.*

astronaut / *l'astronaute*

An **astronaut** is someone who travels out into space.

*Un **astronaute** voyage dans l'espace.*

axe / *la hache*

An **axe** is a sharp tool for cutting wood. Jack cut down the beanstalk with an **axe**.

*Une **hache** est un outil tranchant pour couper le bois. Jacques a coupé la tige de haricot avec une **hache**.*

Bb

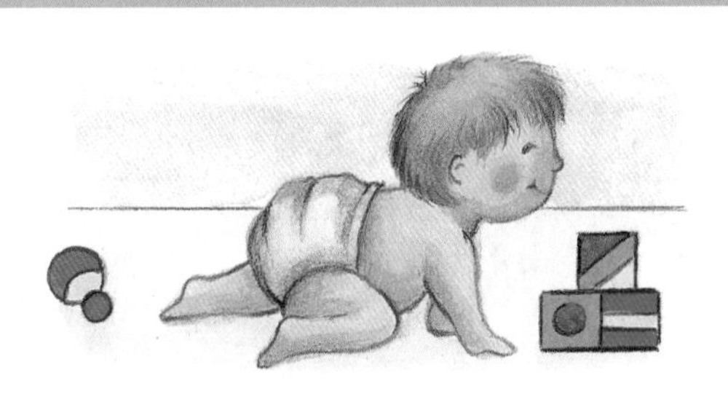

baby / *le bébé*
A **baby** is a very young child.
*Un **bébé** est un très jeune enfant.*

back / *le dos*
The children are standing **back** to **back**.
*Les enfants sont **dos** à **dos**.*

badge / *le badge*
The boy has a **badge** on his jumper.
*Le garçon porte un **badge** sur son chandail.*

bag / *le sac*
You can carry lots of things in a **bag**.
*Tu peux porter beaucoup de choses dans un **sac**.*

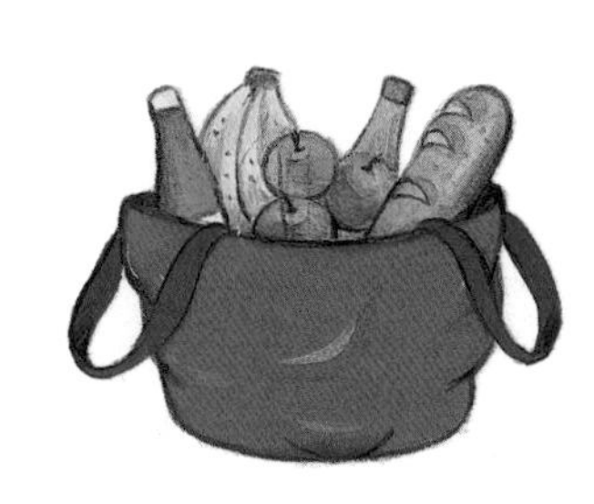

ball / *la balle / le ballon*

Some games are played with a **ball**.

*On joue à certains jeux avec une **balle** ou un **ballon**.*

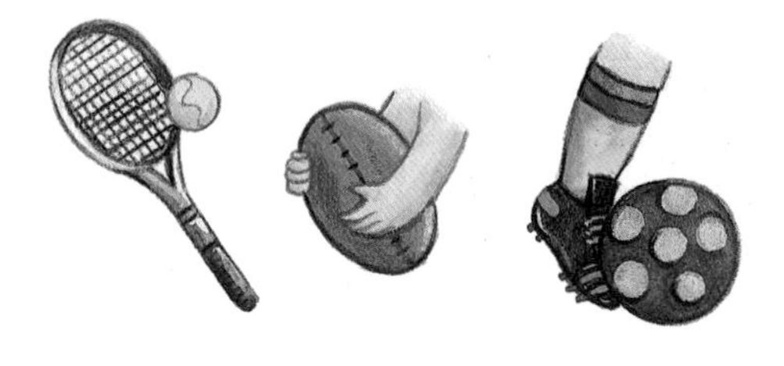

balloon / *ballon*

We blow a **balloon** full of air at parties.

*On gonfle un **ballon** aux fêtes.*

banana / *la banane*

A **banana** is a fruit. We peel off the yellow skin before we eat a **banana**.

*La **banane** est un fruit. Nous épluchons la peau jaune avant de manger une **banane**.*

band / *la fanfare*

A **band** is a group of people who make music together.

*Une **fanfare** est un groupe de personnes jouant de la musique ensemble.*

barn / *la grange*

Farmers keep their cows and hay in a **barn**.

*Les fermiers gardent leurs vaches et leur paille dans une **grange**.*

basket / *le panier*

The man has a large **basket** of flowers.

*L'homme a un grand **panier** de fleurs.*

bat / *la chauve-souris*

This flying animal is a **bat**.

*Cet animal volant est une **chauve-souris**.*

bat / *la batte*

In some games, we hit a ball with a **bat**.

*Dans certain jeux, nous frappons une balle avec une **batte**.*

bath / *la baignoire*

We wash ourselves all over in the **bath**.

Nous nous lavons de la tête aux pieds dans la ***baignoire****.*

beach / *la plage*

The sandy part beside the sea is called the **beach**.

Le rivage sablonneux le long de la mer s'appelle la ***plage****.*

bear / *l'ours*

A **bear** is a large, wild animal.

Un ***ours*** *est un gros animal sauvage.*

bed / *le lit*

We lie down in a **bed** when we want to sleep.

*Nous nous allongeons dans un **lit** lorsque nous voulons dormir.*

bee / *l'abeille*

A **bee** is an insect which lives in a hive and makes honey.

*Une **abeille** est un insecte qui habite dans une ruche et fabrique du miel.*

bell / *la cloche*

A **bell** rings when it is time to go to school.

*Une **cloche** sonne lorsqu'il est l'heure d'aller à l'école.*

berry / *la baie*

A **berry** is a juicy fruit.

*Une **baie** est un fruit juteux.*

bicycle / *la bicyclette*

We can ride a **bicycle**. A **bicycle** has two wheels.

*Nous pouvons rouler à **bicyclette**. Une **bicyclette** a deux roues.*

bird / *l'oiseau*

A **bird** is an animal with wings and feathers. Most **birds** can fly. Here are some **birds**.

*Un **oiseau** est un animal avec des ailes et des plumes. La plupart des **oiseaux** peuvent voler. Voici quelques **oiseaux**.*

black / *le noir*

Black is a very dark colour. The hat is **black**.

*Le **noir** est une couleur très foncée. Le chapeau est **noir**.*

blue / *le bleu*

Blue is a colour. The sky and the ballons are **blue**.

*Le **bleu** est une couleur. Le ciel et les ballons sont **bleus**.*

boat / *le bateau*

You travel over water in a **boat**. The children are in a rowing **boat**.

*Tu voyages sur l'eau dans un **bateau**. Les enfants sont dans un **bateau** à rames.*

book / *le livre*

This girl is reading a **book**. This dictionary is a **book**.

*Cette fille lit un **livre**. Ce dictionnaire est un **livre**.*

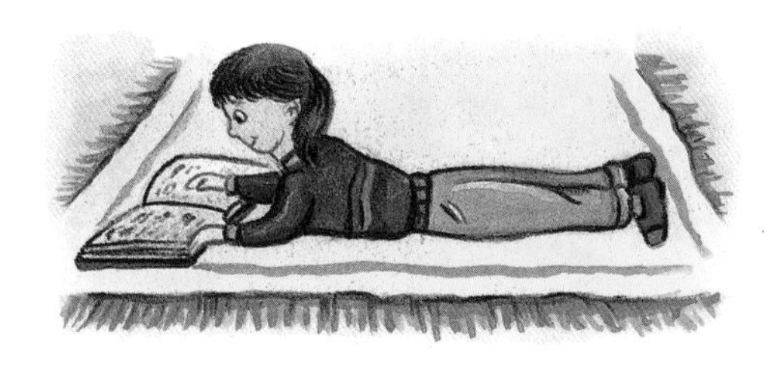

boot / *la botte*

A **boot** covers the foot and part of the leg.

*Une **botte** couvre le pied et une partie de la jambe.*

bottle / *la bouteille*

A **bottle** holds something wet, like water or milk.

*Une **bouteille** contient quelque chose de liquide, comme de l'eau ou du lait.*

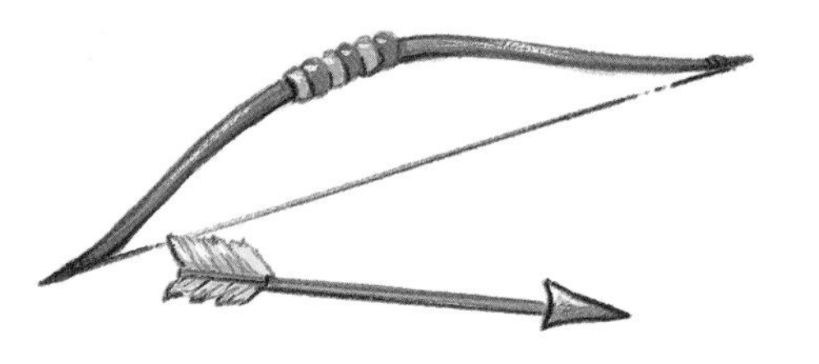

bow / *l'arc*

We use a **bow** for shooting arrows.

*Nous utilisons un **arc** pour tirer des flèches.*

boy \ *le garçon*

A male child is a **boy**.

*Un enfant mâle est un **garçon**.*

bridge / *le pont*

We use a **bridge** to cross over a road or a river.

*Nous utilisons un **pont** pour passer au-dessus d'une route ou d'une rivière.*

brown / *le marron*

Brown is a colour. The coat and the teddy are **brown**.

*Le **marron** est une couleur. Le manteau et l'ours en peluche sont **marron**.*

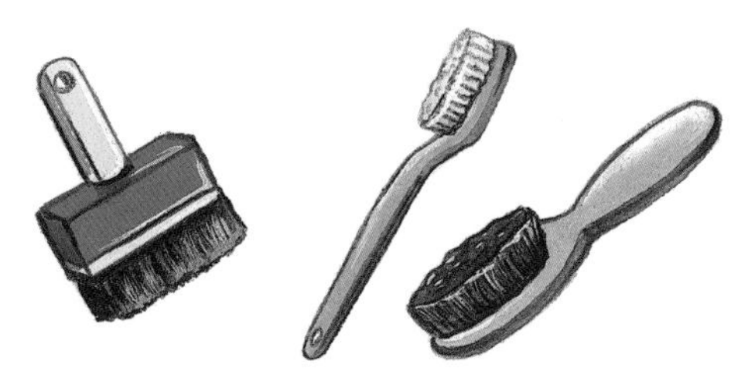

brush / *la brosse / le pinceau*

We use a **brush** for painting or cleaning. We **brush** our hair.

*Nous utilisons un **pinceau** pour peindre et une **brosse** pour nettoyer. Nous nous **brossons** les cheveux.*

bulldozer / *le bulldozer*

A **bulldozer** can move piles of earth or rubble.

*Un **bulldozer** peut déplacer de la terre ou des débris.*

bus / *l'autobus*

A **bus** can carry people along the road.

*Un **autobus** peut transporter des gens sur la route.*

butterfly / *le papillon*

A **butterfly** is an insect with four large wings.

*Un **papillon** est un insecte avec quatre grandes ailes.*

Cc

cage / *la cage*

We keep pet birds or mice in a **cage**.

*Nous gardons des oiseaux ou des souris de compagnie en **cage**.*

cake / *le gâteau*

A **cake** is sweet and baked in the oven.

*Un **gâteau** est sucré et cuit au four.*

camel / *le chameau*

A **camel** is an animal with one or two humps which lives in the desert.

*Un **chameau** est un animal à une ou deux bosses qui vit dans le désert.*

candle / *la bougie*

A **candle** gives us light.

*Une **bougie** nous donne de la lumière.*

car / *la voiture*

We travel by **car** along the road.

*Nous voyageons en **voiture** sur la route.*

castle / *le château*

A **castle** is an old building with thick walls and towers.

*Un **château** est un vieux bâtiment avec des murs épais et des tours.*

cat / *le chat*

A **cat** is a furry animal. We keep **cats** as pets.

*Un **chat** est un animal à poils. Les **chats** sont des animaux de compagnie.*

caterpillar / *la chenille*

A **caterpillar** has lots of legs and changes into a moth or a butterfly.

*Une **chenille** a beaucoup de pattes et se transforme en papillon de jour ou de nuit.*

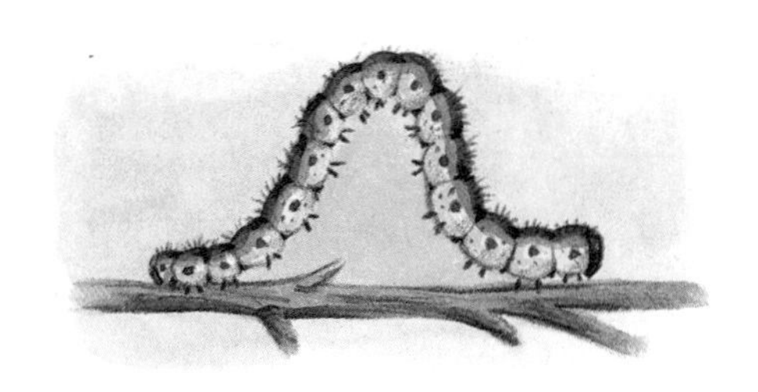

cherry / *la cerise*

A **cherry** is a small, round, tasty fruit. **Cherries** are good to eat.

*Une **cerise** est un petit fruit rond et délicieux. **Les cerises** ont bon goût.*

chicken / *le poulet*

A **chicken** is a bird. These baby **chickens** are called chicks.

*Un **poulet** est un oiseau. Ces bébés **poulets** s'appellent des poussins.*

chimney / *la cheminée*

The smoke from the fire goes up the **chimney**.

*La fumée du feu sort par la **cheminée**.*

Christmas / *Noël*

December 25th is **Christmas**, the birthday of Jesus. We give presents at **Christmas**.

*Le 25 décembre c'est **Noël**, l'anniversaire de Jésus. Nous offrons des cadeaux à **Noël**.*

clock / *le réveil*

A **clock** shows us the time.

*Un **réveil** nous indique l'heure*

clothes / *les vêtements*

All the things we wear are called **clothes**.

*Toutes les choses que nous portons s'appellent des **vêtements**.*

cot / *le lit d'enfant*

A baby sleeps in a little bed called a **cot**.

*Un bébé dort dans un petit lit que l'on appelle un **lit d'enfant**.*

cow / *la vache*

A **cow** is an animal that gives us milk.

*Une **vache** est un animal qui nous donne du lait.*

crab / *le crabe*

A **crab** lives in the sea. **Crabs** can nip you with their claws.

*Un **crabe** vit dans la mer. Les **crabes** peuvent te pincer avec leurs pinces.*

crane / *la grue*

A **crane** is a machine which lifts large, heavy things.

*Une **grue** est une machine qui peut soulever des gros objets lourds*

crayon / *le crayon de couleur*

We can use a **crayon** to colour a drawing.

*Nous pouvons utiliser un **crayon de couleur** pour colorier un dessin.*

cup / *la tasse*

We drink something out of a **cup**.

*Nous buvons quelque chose dans une **tasse**.*

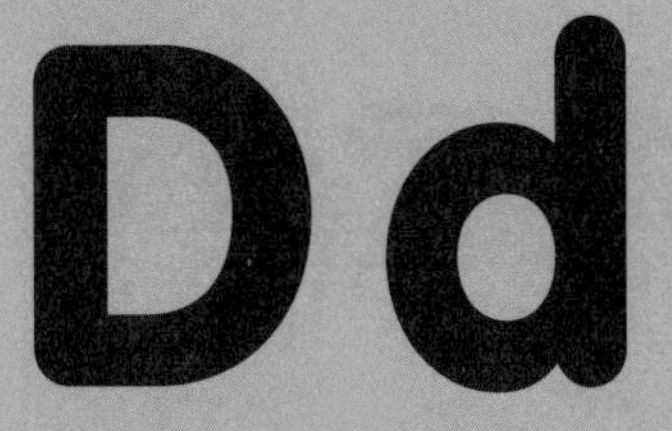

dancer / *le danseur / la danseuse*

A **dancer** moves about in time to music.

*Une **danseuse** bouge en suivant la musique.*

deer / *le daim*

Deer are shy, wild animals.

*Les **daims** sont des animaux sauvages timides.*

dentist / *le dentiste*

A **dentist** is someone who helps us to keep our teeth shining and healthy.

*Un **dentiste** est une personne qui nous aide à garder nos dents brillantes et en bonne santé.*

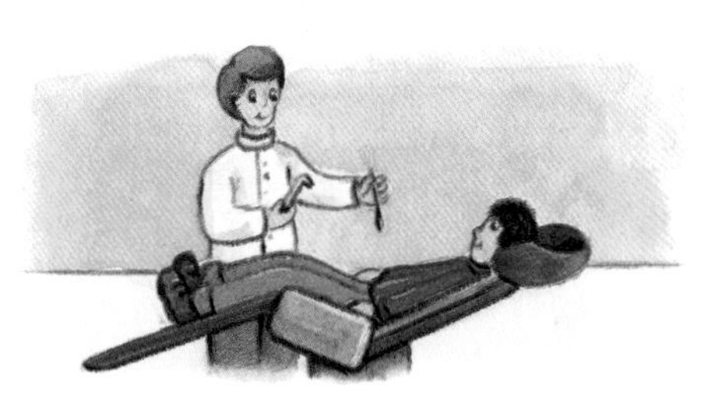

desk / *le bureau*

We can sit at a **desk** when we want to read or write.

*Nous pouvons nous asseoir à un **bureau** lorsque nous voulons lire ou écrire.*

dice / *le dé*

We use a **dice** to play some games. A **dice** has six sides.

*Nous utilisons un **dé** pour jouer à certains jeux. Un **dé** a six côtés.*

dinosaur / *le dinosaure*

A **dinosaur** is an animal that lived a long, long time ago. Some **dinosaurs** were big and fierce.

*Un **dinosaure** est un animal qui vivait il y a très, très longtemps. Certains **dinosaures** étaient grands et féroces.*

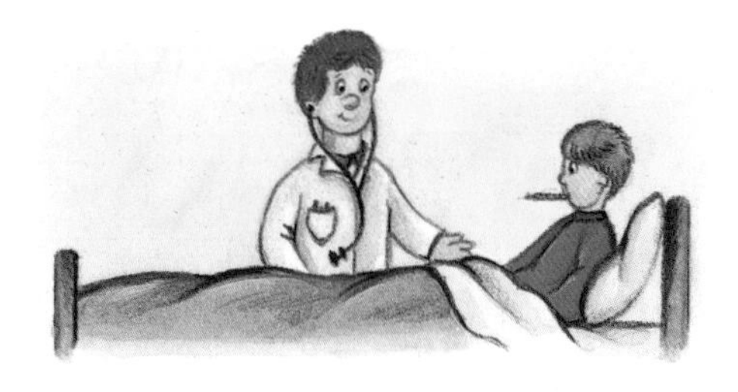

doctor / *le docteur*

When we are sick, a **doctor** will take care of us.

*Lorsque nous sommes malades, un **docteur** s'occupe de nous.*

dog / *le chien*

A **dog** is a friend. Some **dogs** are big, and some are small.

*Le **chien** est un ami. Certains **chiens** sont grands, et d'autres sont petits.*

doll / *la poupée*

A **doll** is a toy that looks like a person.

*Une **poupée** est un jouet qui ressemble à une personne.*

donkey / *l'âne*

A **donkey** is an animal with long ears. **Donkeys** say : "Hee-Haw".

*Un **âne** est un animal à longues oreilles. Les **ânes** font : «hi-han».*

door / *la porte*

A room or a cupboard has a **door**. We can open and close a **door**.

*Une pièce ou une armoire a une **porte**. Nous pouvons ouvrir et fermer une **porte**.*

dragon / *le dragon*

In fairy tales, a **dragon** is a fire-breathing animal with wings.

*Dans les contes de fées, un **dragon** est un animal qui crache le feu et qui a des ailes.*

dress / *la robe*

A girl or a woman will wear a **dress**.

*Les filles et les femmes portent des **robes**.*

drum / *le tambour*

We can make music with a **drum** by hitting it with **drum**sticks

*Nous pouvons faire de la musique en tapant sur un **tambour** avec des baguettes.*

duck / *le canard*

A **duck** is a bird that can swim and fly.

*Un **canard** est un oiseau qui peut nager et voler.*

Ee

eagle / *l'aigle*

An **eagle** is a big bird with strong claws.

*Un **aigle** est un grand oiseau avec de grosses serres.*

ear / *l'oreille*

On each side of our head, we have an **ear**. We hear with our **ears**.

*De chaque côté de notre tête, nous avons une **oreille**. Nous entendons avec nos **oreilles**.*

eggs / *les œufs*

Birds and some other animals lay **eggs**. We can eat some **eggs**.

*Les oiseaux et certains autres animaux pondent des **œufs**. Nous pouvons manger certains **œufs**.*

elbow / *le coude*

Our arms bend in the middle at the **elbow**.

*Nos bras se plient en deux au **coude**.*

elephant / *l'éléphant*

An **elephant** is a large, grey animal with big ears, and a very long nose, called a trunk.

Un ***éléphant*** *est un gros animal gris avec de grandes oreilles et un très long nez, que l'on appelle une trompe.*

empty / *vide*

The box is **empty**. There is nothing in the box.

La boîte est ***vide****. Il n'y a rien dans la boîte.*

end / *le bout*

The **end** is the last of something. Each dog has an **end** of the rope.

Le ***bout*** *est la fin de quelque chose. Chaque chien tient un* ***bout*** *de la corde.*

envelope / *l'enveloppe*

When we have written a letter, we put it into an **envelope** before we post it.

Lorsque nous avons écrit une lettre, nous la mettons dans une ***enveloppe*** *avant de la poster.*

Eskimo / *l'Eskimo*

An **Eskimo** lives in a very cold part of the world. **Eskimos** have to wear warm, furry clothes.

*Un **Eskimo** habite dans un endroit très froid du monde. Les **Eskimos** portent des vêtements chauds en fourrure.*

exercises / *les exercices*

The children are doing **exercises**. **Exercises** are special movements to keep our bodies fit.

*Les enfants font des **exercices**. Les **exercices** sont des mouvements spéciaux pour maintenir nos corps en forme.*

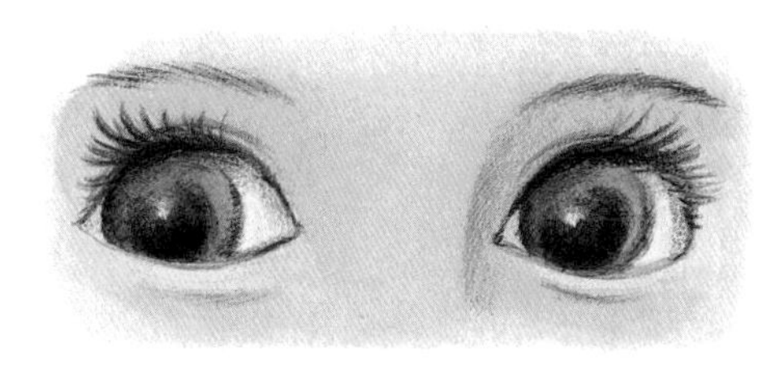

eye / *l'œil*

The **eye** is the part of our body through which we see. We have two **eyes**.

*L'**œil** est la partie du corps par laquelle nous voyons. Nous avons deux **yeux**.*

face / *le visage*

The **face** is on the front of the head.

*Le **visage** se trouve sur le devant de la tête.*

fair / *la foire*

We can have lots of fun at a **fair**.

*Nous pouvons bien nous amuser à la **foire**.*

farm / *la ferme*

On a **farm**, food is grown and **farm** animals are kept.

*A la **ferme**, on fait pousser de la nourriture et on élève des animaux de **ferme**.*

feather / *la plume*

A **feather** is very light. **Feathers** grow on birds.

*Une **plume** est très légère. Les **plumes** poussent sur les oiseaux.*

fence / *la clôture*

You put a **fence** of wood or wire round your garden.

*Tu mets une **clôture** en bois ou en fil de fer autour de ton jardin.*

finger / *le doigt*

A **finger** is a part of the hand. We have eight **fingers** and two thumbs.

*Un **doigt** fait partie de la main. Nous avons huit **doigts** et deux pouces.*

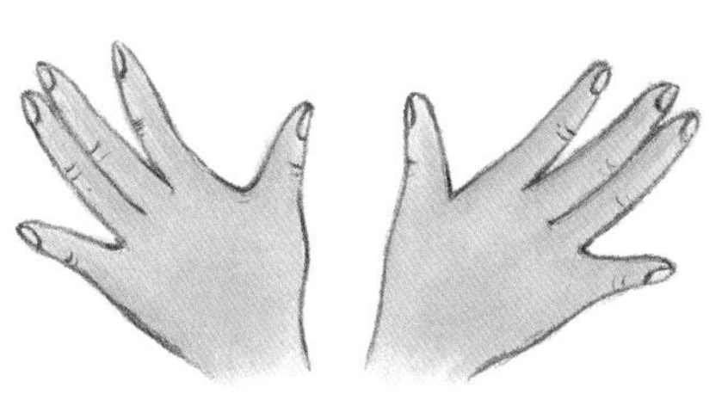

fire / *le feu*

When something is burning, there is a **fire**. A **fire** is very hot.

*Lorsque quelque chose brûle, il y a un **feu**. Un **feu** est très chaud.*

fish / *poisson*

A **fish** is an animal that lives in the water.

*Un **poisson** est un animal qui vit dans l'eau.*

flag / *le drapeau*

A **flag** is a coloured piece of cloth or paper. This is the pirates' **flag**.

*Un **drapeau** est un morceau de tissu ou de papier en couleur. Voici le **drapeau** des pirates.*

flowers / *les fleurs*

Flowers are pretty and they smell nice. A **flower** is the part of a plant with seeds in it.

*Les **fleurs** sont jolies et elles sentent bon. La **fleur** est la partie d'une plante qui contient des graines.*

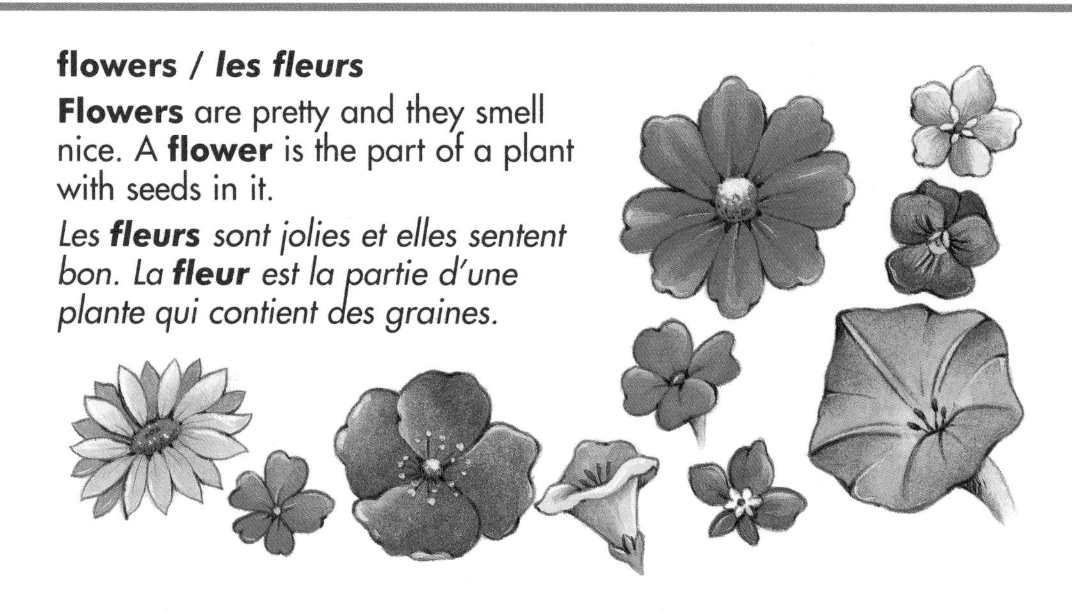

food / *la nourriture*

Food is what we eat. Everything needs **food** to stay alive.

*La **nourriture** est ce que nous mangeons. Tout a besoin de **nourriture** pour rester en vie.*

foot / *le pied*

At the end of each leg, we have a **foot**. We stand on our **feet**.

*Au bout de chaque jambe, nous avons un **pied**. Nous nous tenons debout sur nos **pieds**.*

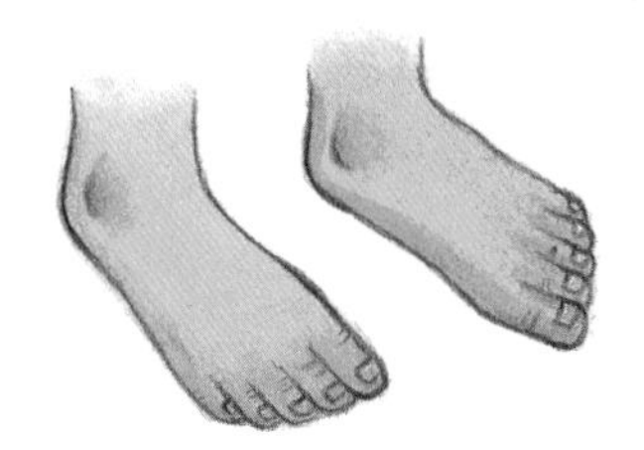

forest / *la forêt*

There are lots of trees in a **forest**.

*Il y a beaucoup d'arbres dans une **forêt**.*

fountain / *la fontaine*

A **fountain** shoots water up into the air.

*Une **fontaine** lance de l'eau en l'air.*

fox / *le renard*

A **fox** is a kind of wild dog, with a bushy tail.

*Un **renard** est un genre de chien sauvage, avec une queue touffue.*

frog / *la grenouille*

A **frog** is a small animal that lives near water. **Frogs** jump and have webbed feet.

*Une **grenouille** est un petit animal qui vit près de l'eau. Les **grenouilles** sautent et ont des pattes palmées.*

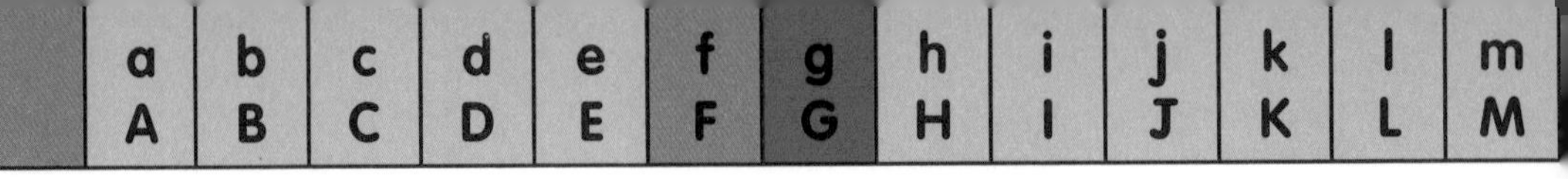

fruit / *le fruit*

Some plants have **fruit**. We eat **fruit**, like oranges, bananas and strawberries.

*Certaines plantes ont des **fruits**. Nous mangeons des **fruits**, comme les oranges, les bananes et les fraises.*

full / *plein*

When you cannot get any more into something, it is **full**.

*Lorsque tu ne peux plus rien mettre dans quelque chose, c'est **plein**.*

funny / *amusant*

The clown makes the children laugh. They think the clown is **funny**.

*Le clown fait rire les enfants. Ils trouvent que le clown est **amusant**.*

garage / *le garage*
The car is in the **garage**.
La voiture est dans le ***garage****.*

garden / *le jardin*
We grow grass and flowers in a **garden**. We can play in the **garden**.
Nous faisons pousser de l'herbe et des fleurs dans un ***jardin****. Nous pouvons jouer dans le* ***jardin****.*

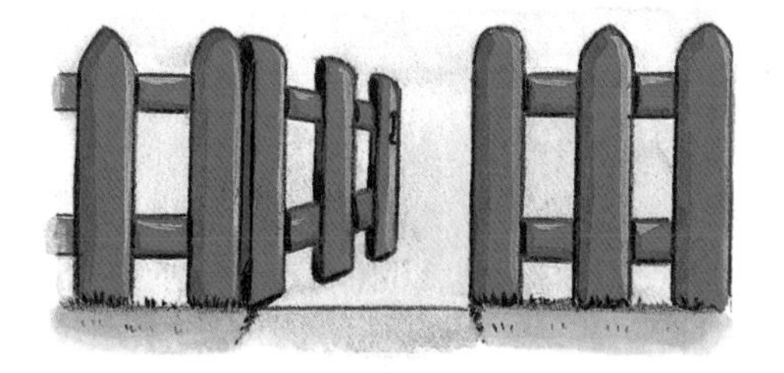

gate / *la grille*
A **gate** is like a door in a fence.
Une ***grille*** *est comme une porte dans une clôture.*

giant / *le géant*

A **giant** is a very big person in a fairy tale.

*Un **géant** est une très grande personne dans un conte de fées.*

giraffe / *la girafe*

A **giraffe** is a wild animal with long legs and a very long neck.

*Une **girafe** est un animal sauvage avec de longues jambes et un très long cou.*

girl / *la fille*

A female child is a **girl**.

*Un enfant femelle est une **fille**.*

gloves / *les gants*

We wear **gloves** to keep our hands warm.

*Nous portons des **gants** pour avoir chaud aux mains.*

goat / *la chèvre*

A **goat** is like a large sheep with horns and a beard.

*Une **chèvre** ressemble à un gros mouton avec des cornes et une barbe.*

goldfish / *le poisson rouge*

We keep **goldfish** as pets in a tank.

*Nous mettons des **poissons** rouges de compagnie dans un aquarium.*

grass / *l'herbe*

Grass is green, and grows almost everywhere. We have to cut the **grass** in the garden.

***L'herbe** est verte et pousse presque partout. Nous devons couper **l'herbe** du jardin.*

green / *le vert*

Green is a colour. The jumper is **green**. So is the scarf.

*Le **vert** est une couleur. Le chandail est **vert**. L'écharpe aussi.*

grey / *le gris*

Grey is a colour. Clouds are **grey** when it is raining.

*Le **gris** est une couleur. Les nuages sont **gris** quand il pleut.*

Hh

hammer / *le marteau*

A **hammer** is a tool for banging in nails.

*Un **marteau** est un outil pour enfoncer les clous.*

hamster / *le hamster*

A **hamster** is a small, furry animal. **Hamsters** keep food in their cheeks.

*Un **hamster** est un petit animal à poils. Les **hamsters** gardent leur nourriture dans leurs joues.*

hand / *la main*

We have a **hand** at the end of each arm. Our **hands** are for holding and touching things.

*Nous avons une **main** au bout de chaque bras. Nos **mains** nous servent à tenir et à toucher les choses.*

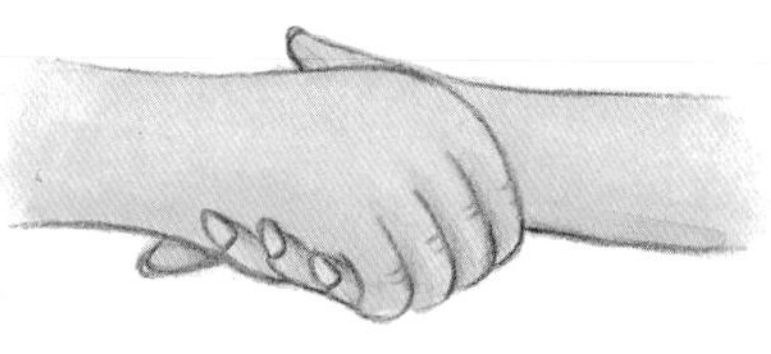

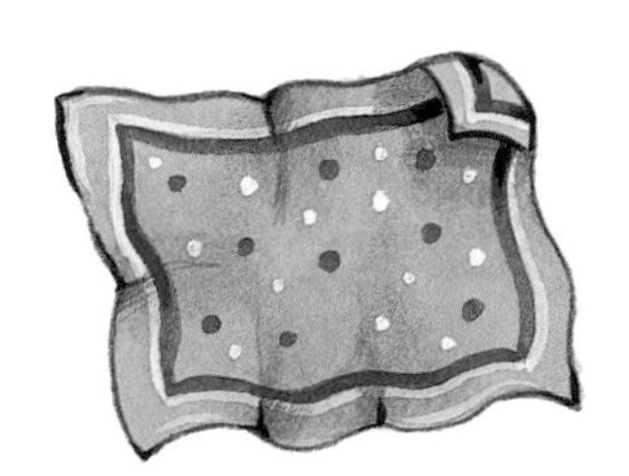

handkerchief / *le mouchoir*

We use a **handkerchief** to wipe our nose when we have a cold.

*Nous utilisons un **mouchoir** pour nous moucher quand nous avons un rhume.*

harp / *la harpe*

We pluck the strings on a **harp** to make music.

*Nous pinçons les cordes d'une **harpe** pour jouer de la musique.*

hat / *le chapeau*

We wear a **hat** on our head. This is a man's **hat**.

*Nous portons un **chapeau** sur la tête. Voici un **chapeau** d'homme.*

hay / *la paille*

Hay is dried grass and is used for feeding cows and sheep.

*La **paille** est de l'herbe séchée qui sert à nourrir les vaches et les moutons.*

head / *la tête*

Our **head** is on our shoulders. The face is the front of the **head**.

*Notre **tête** se trouve sur nos épaules. Le visage est le devant de la **tête**.*

hedge / *la haie*

A **hedge** is a row of bushes which makes a fence round a field.

*Une **haie** est une ligne de buissons qui forme une clôture autour d'un champ.*

heel / *le talon*

The **heel** is the back part of the foot.

*Le **talon** est la partie arrière du pied.*

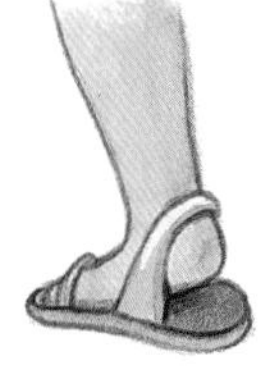

helicopter / *l'hélicoptère*

A **helicopter** is an aircraft without wings which can fly straight up into the air.

*Un **hélicoptère** est un avion sans ailes qui peut s'élever tout droit dans l'air.*

helmet / *le casque*

A **helmet** is a strong cover for the head. We wear a **helmet** to keep our head safe.

*Un **casque** est une protection solide pour la tête. Nous portons un **casque** pour protéger notre tête.*

hen / *la poule*

A female bird is called a **hen**. We can eat the eggs of **hens**.

*La femelle de certains oiseaux s'appelle une **poule**. Nous pouvons manger les oeufs des **poules**.*

hill / *la colline*

A **hill** is higher than the land around it. **Hills** are not as high as mountains.

*Une **colline** est plus élevée que le terrain autour. Les **collines** ne sont pas aussi élevées que les montagnes.*

hook / *le portemanteau*

We can hang a coat on a **hook**.

Nous pouvons accrocher un manteau à un ***portemanteau****.*

horn / *la corne / le bois*

Horns are the pointed bits on the heads of deer. A rhino has a **horn** on its nose.

Les ***bois*** *sont les morceaux pointus sur la tête des cerfs. Un rhinocéros a une* ***corne*** *sur son museau.*

horse / *le cheval*

A **horse** is an animal which is used for riding, or for pulling carts.

Un ***cheval*** *est un animal que l'on monte ou qui tire des chariots.*

hospital / *l'hôpital*

When we are very sick, we have to go to **hospital**.

Lorsque nous sommes très malades, nous devons aller à ***l'hôpital****.*

Ii

iceberg / *l'iceberg*

A very large block of ice which floats in the sea is an **iceberg**.

*Un très gros morceau de glace qui flotte dans la mer s'appelle un **iceberg**.*

ice cream / *la crème glacée*

Ice cream is cold and sweet. Eating **ice cream** is great.

*La **crème glacée** est froide et sucrée. Manger de la **crème glacée** est agréable.*

icicles / *les stalactites*

Icicles are pointed spikes of frozen water.

*Les **stalactites** sont des aiguilles d'eau gelée.*

icing / *le glaçage*

Icing is the sweet topping put on birthday cakes.

*Le **glaçage** est la garniture sucrée des gâteaux d'anniversaire.*

igloo / *l'igloo*

Eskimos live in houses called **igloos**, made from frozen snow.

*Les Eskimos habitent des maisons que l'on appelle des **igloos**, construits avec de la neige gelée.*

insects / *les insectes*

Insects are small animals with six legs. Some **insects** are small, some are big.

*Les **insectes** sont de petits animaux à six pattes. Certains **insectes** sont petits, d'autres sont gros.*

iron / *le fer à repasser*

We press clothes with an **iron**.

*Nous repassons les vêtements avec un **fer à repasser**.*

island / *l'île*

An **island** is a piece of land with water all around it.

*Une **île** est un morceau de terre entouré d'eau.*

Jj

jack-in-the-box / *le diable à ressort*

When you open the lid of a **jack-in-the-box**, a toy jumps out.

*Lorsque tu ouvres le couvercle d'un **diable à ressort**, un jouet en sort.*

jar / *le pot*

We can keep sweets in a **jar**.

*Nous pouvons ranger des bonbons dans un **pot**.*

jeans / *le jean*

Jeans are trousers made from strong blue cloth.

*Un **jean** est un pantalon de tissu bleu très solide.*

jelly / *la gelée*

Jelly is a cold, clear, sweet pudding.

*La **gelée** est un dessert froid, clair et sucré.*

jellyfish / *la méduse*

A **jellyfish** lives in the sea. Jellyfish look as if they are made of jelly.

*La **méduse** vit dans la mer. On dirait que les méduses sont faites de gelée.*

jigsaw / *le puzzle*

We have to fit together the pieces of a **jigsaw** puzzle.

*Nous devons mettre ensemble les morceaux d'un **puzzle**.*

juggler / *le jongleur*

A **juggler** throws and catches lots of things all at once.

*Un **jongleur** lance et attrape beaucoup de choses à la fois.*

jumper / *le chandail*

A knitted pullover with long sleeves is a **jumper**.

*Un tricot à longues manches s'appelle un **chandail**.*

kangaroo / *le kangourou*

A **kangaroo** is an Australian animal which carries its baby in a pouch.

*Le **kangourou** est un animal australien qui transporte son bébé dans une poche.*

key / *la clé*

You open a lock with a **key**.

*Tu ouvres une serrure avec une **clé**.*

king / *le roi*

A **king** is the head of a country.

*Le **roi** est le chef d'un pays.*

kiss / *le baiser*

The girl is giving the baby a **kiss**.

*La fille donne un **baiser** au bébé.*

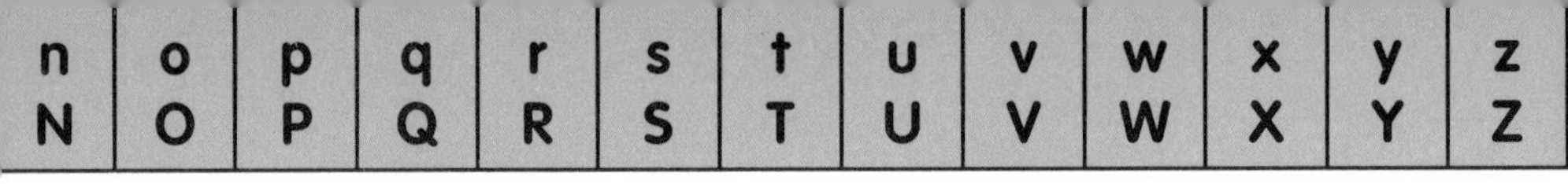

kite / *le cerf-volant*

The boy is flying a **kite**. He must hold on to the string of his **kite**.

*Le garçon fait voler un **cerf-volant**. Il doit tenir la ficelle de son **cerf-volant**.*

kitten / *le chaton*

A **kitten** is a young cat.

*Un **chaton** est un jeune chat.*

knee / *le genou*

Your leg bends in the middle of the **knee**.

*Ta jambe se plie en deux au **genou**.*

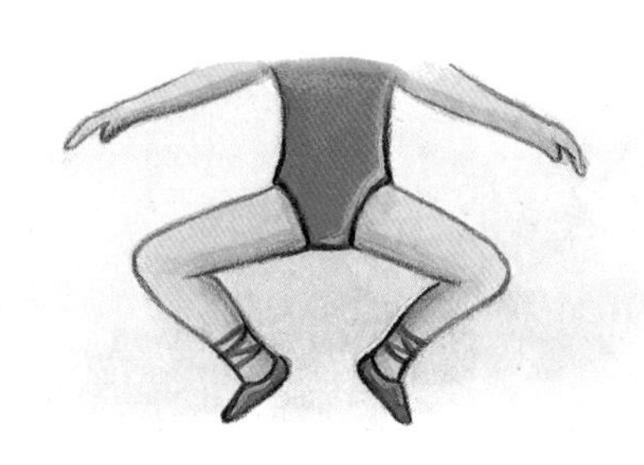

knife / *le couteau*

We cut things with a **knife**.

*Nous coupons des choses avec un **couteau**.*

Ll

ladder / *l'échelle*

You climb a **ladder** to get up to high things.

*Tu montes à **l'échelle** pour atteindre des choses élevées.*

ladybird / *la coccinelle*

A **ladybird** is a red or yellow insect with spots on its back.

*Une **coccinelle** est un insecte rouge ou jaune avec des taches sur le dos.*

lake / *le lac*

A **lake** is a lot of water with land all round it.

*Un **lac** est une grande étendue d'eau entourée de terre.*

lamb / *l'agneau*
A **lamb** is a young sheep.
*Un **agneau** est un jeune mouton.*

lamp / *la lampe*
A **lamp** gives us light. When it gets dark, we switch on the **lamp**.
*Une **lampe** donne de la lumière. Lorsqu'il fait noir, nous allumons la **lampe**.*

leaf / *la feuille*
A **leaf** will grow on a tree or a plant.
*Une **feuille** pousse sur un arbre ou une plante.*

leap-frog / *le saute-mouton*
It is fun to play **leap-frog**.
In **leap-frog**, you leap over your friends' backs.
*C'est amusant de jouer à **saute-mouton**.*
*Au **saute-mouton**, tu sautes par-dessus le dos de tes amis.*

leg / *la jambe*

We have two **legs**. The boy is waving one **leg** in the air.

*Nous avons deux **jambes**. Le garçon secoue une **jambe** en l'air.*

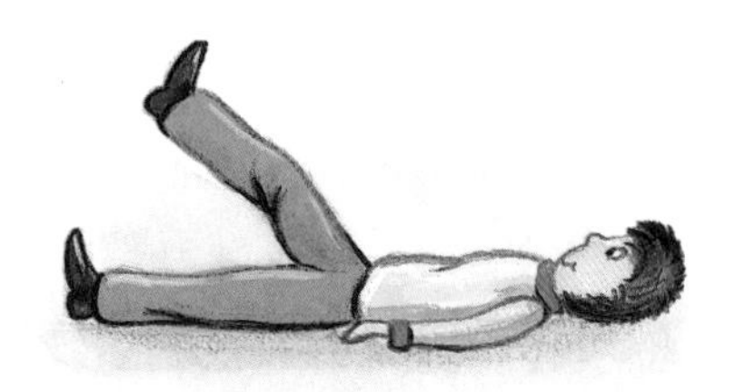

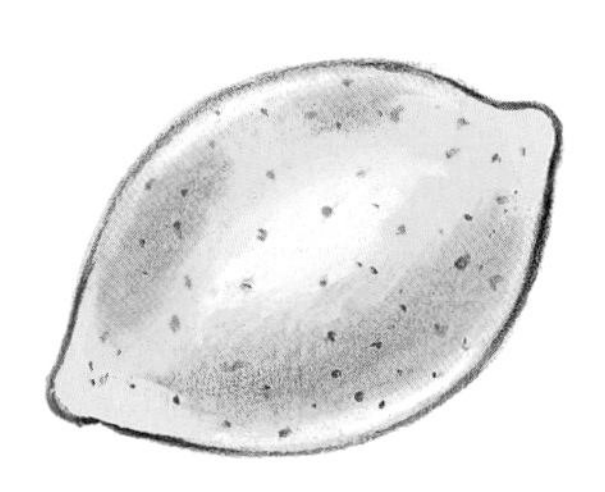

lemon / le *citron*

A **lemon** is a yellow fruit with a bitter taste.

*Le **citron** est un fruit jaune au goût sur.*

leopard / *le léopard*

A **leopard** is a large, wild animal with a spotted coat.

*Le **léopard** est un grand animal sauvage à fourrure tachetée.*

letter / *la lettre*

When we write a **letter**, we are sending a message to someone.

*Lorsque nous écrivons une **lettre**, nous envoyons un message à quelqu'un.*

library / *la bibliothèque*

A **library** is a room or a building where books are kept.

*Une **bibliothèque** est une pièce ou un bâtiment où l'on range les livres.*

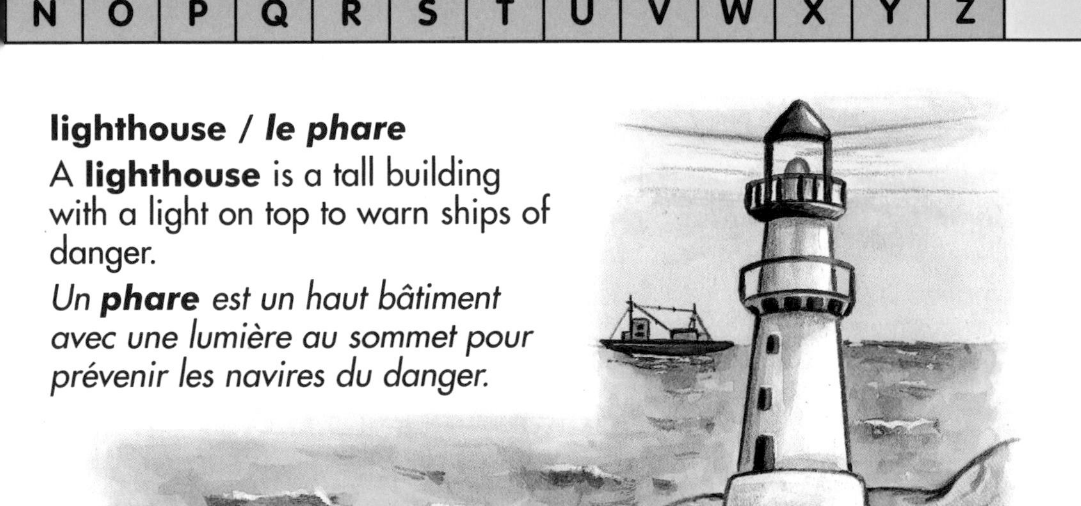

lighthouse / *le phare*

A **lighthouse** is a tall building with a light on top to warn ships of danger.

*Un **phare** est un haut bâtiment avec une lumière au sommet pour prévenir les navires du danger.*

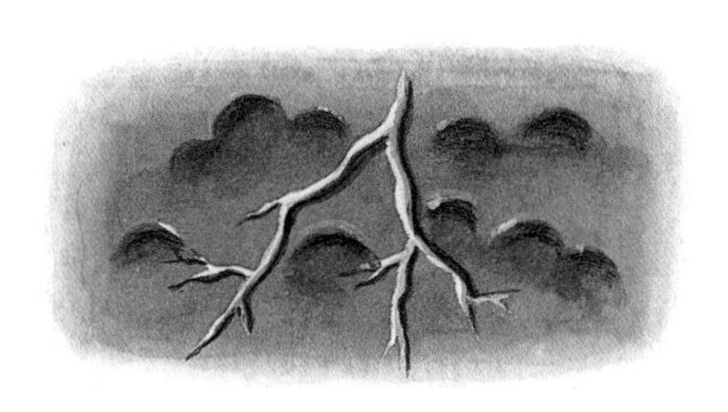

lightning / *l'éclair*

Lightning is the flash that we see in the sky during a thunderstorm.

***L'éclair** est la lumière que nous voyons dans le ciel durant un orage.*

lion / *le lion*

A **lion** is a fierce, wild animal. **Lions** are part of the cat family.

*Un **lion** est un animal sauvage féroce. Les **lions** font partie de la famille des chats.*

lizard / *le lézard*

A **lizard** is an animal with short legs and a long tail.

*Un **lézard** est un animal à courtes pattes et à longue queue.*

lock / *le cadenas*

The cupboard has a **lock** on it. You need a key to un**lock** the cupboard.

*Il y a un **cadenas** sur l'armoire. Tu as besoin d'une clé pour ouvrir l'armoire.*

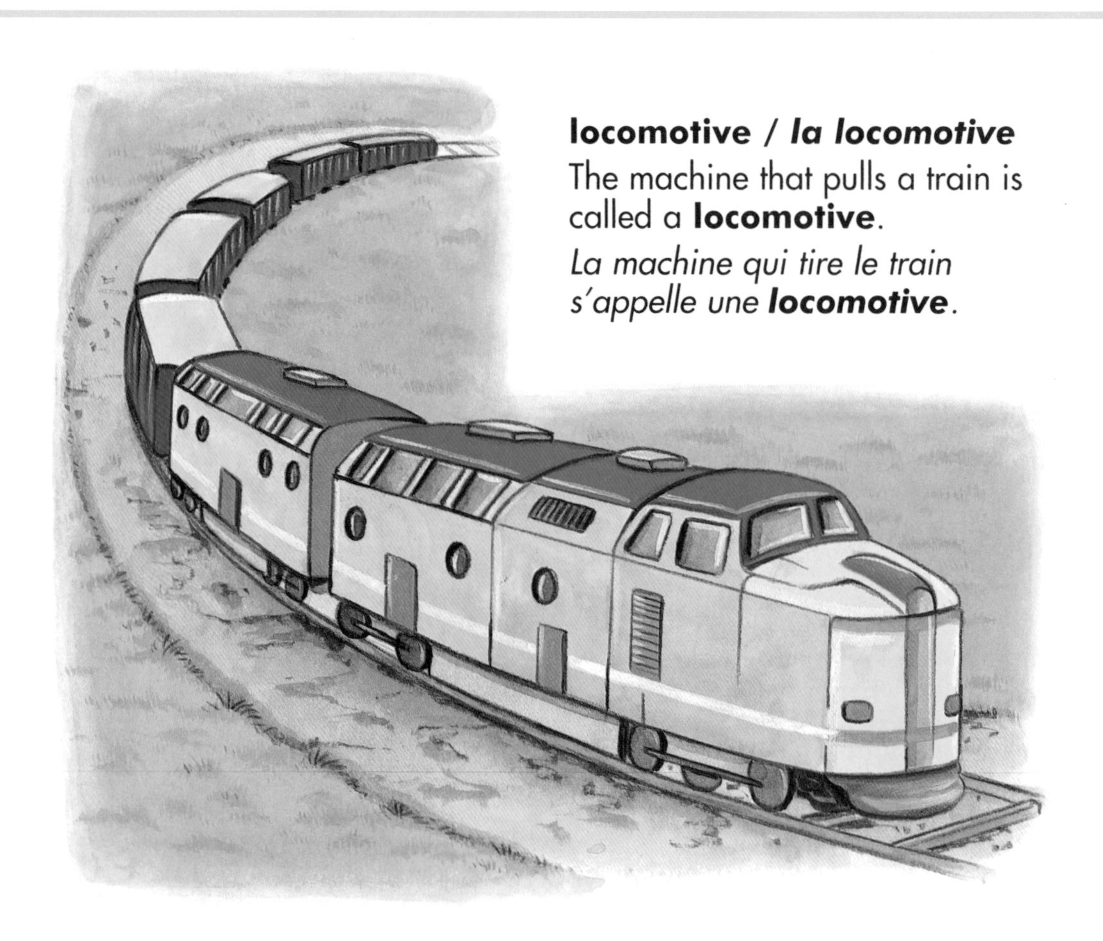

locomotive / *la locomotive*

The machine that pulls a train is called a **locomotive**.

*La machine qui tire le train s'appelle une **locomotive**.*

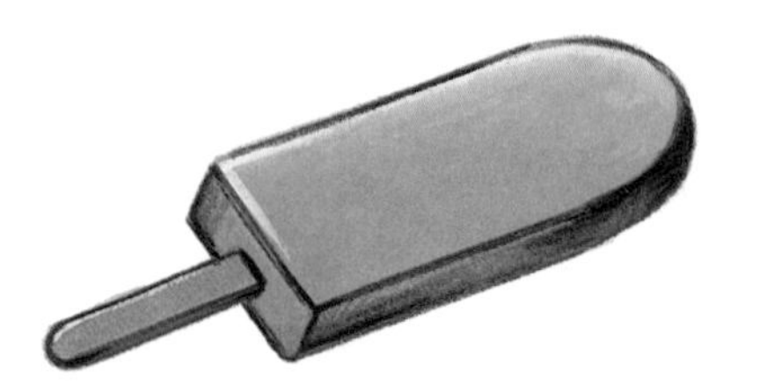

lollipop / *la sucette*

A **lollipop** is a sweet on a stick. We lick a **lollipop**.

*Une **sucette** est un bonbon sur un bâton. On suce une **sucette**.*

Mm

machine / *la machine*

A **machine** is something that helps us to do work. We clean clothes in a washing-**machine**.

*Une **machine** est quelque chose qui nous aide à faire notre travail. Nous nettoyons les vêtements dans une **machine** à laver.*

magic / *la magie*

The man is doing **magic** tricks. It is difficult to understand how a **magic** trick works.

*L'homme fait des tours de **magie**. Il est difficile de comprendre les tours de **magie**.*

mask / *le masque*

The boy is wearing a **mask**. His face is covered with a **mask**.

*Le garçon porte un **masque**. Il a un **masque** sur le visage.*

mat / *le paillasson*

A **mat** is like a small rug. We wipe our feet on a door**mat**.

*Un **paillasson** est un petit tapis. Nous nous essuyons les pieds sur un **paillasson**.*

medicine / *le médicament*

Medicine is something we take to make us better.

*Un **médicament** est quelque chose que nous prenons pour nous soigner.*

mermaid / *la sirène*

In stories, a **mermaid** is a woman who lives in the sea and has a fish's tail.

*Dans les histoires, une **sirène** est une dame qui vit dans la mer et qui a une queue de poisson.*

milk / *le lait*

Milk is a white drink that comes from cows. Children drink a lot of **milk**.

*Le **lait** est un breuvage blanc qui vient des vaches. Les enfants boivent beaucoup de **lait**.*

mirror / *le miroir*

A **mirror** is a piece of glass that we can see ourselves in.

*Un **miroir** est un morceau de verre dans lequel nous pouvons nous voir.*

mole / *la taupe*

A **mole** is a furry animal that lives underground.

*Une **taupe** est un animal à poils qui vit sous la terre.*

moneybox / *la tirelire*

We keep our savings in a **moneybox**.

*Nous gardons nos économies dans une **tirelire**.*

monkey / *le singe*

A **monkey** is a wild, furry animal which is very good at climbing.

*Le **singe** est un animal sauvage à poils qui grimpe très bien.*

mountain / *la montagne*

A hill that is very high is called a **mountain**.

*Une très haute colline s'appelle une **montagne**.*

mouse / *la souris*

A **mouse** is a tiny animal with a long tail and sharp teeth.

*Une **souris** est un tout petit animal à longue queue et à dents pointues.*

mouth / *la bouche*

A **mouth** is the opening in our face. We talk and eat with our mouths.

*La **bouche** est l'ouverture dans notre visage. Nous parlons et mangeons avec notre **bouche**.*

mushroom / *le champignon*

A **mushroom** is a small plant that grows in woods and fields.

*Un **champignon** est une petite plante qui pousse dans les bois et les champs.*

music / *la musique*

Music is the nice sound you make when you sing. Guitar **music** also sounds good.

*La **musique** est le son agréable que tu fais lorsque tu chantes. La guitare fait aussi de la **musique** agréable.*

Nn

neck / *le cou*

The **neck** is the part of the body that joins the head to the shoulders. Giraffes have very long necks.

*Le **cou** est la partie du corps qui relie la tête aux épaules. Les girafes ont de très longs **cous**.*

necklace / *le collier*

Some people wear a decoration round their neck called a **necklace**.

*Certaines personnes portent une décoration autour du cou que l'on appelle un **collier**.*

needle / *l'aiguille*

We use a **needle** for sewing.

*Nous utilisons une **aiguille** pour coudre.*

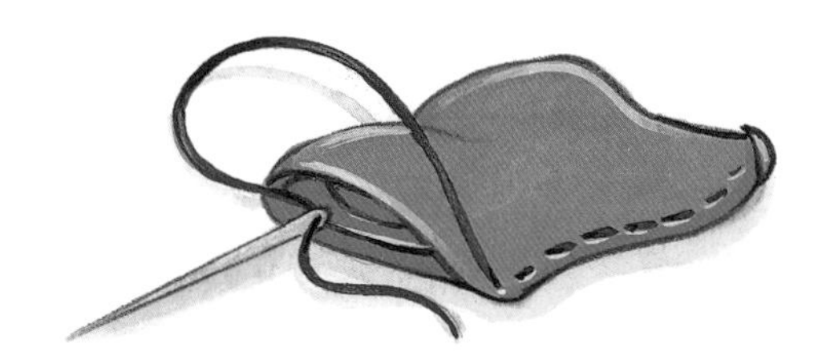

nest / *le nid*

Birds, and some other animals, make a home called a **nest**.

*Les oiseaux, et certains autres animaux, fabriquent des maisons que l'on appelle des **nids**.*

net / *le filet*

Sometimes a **net** is used for catching fish.

*Parfois on utilise un **filet** pour attraper des poissons.*

newt / *la salamandre*

A **newt** is like a lizard that lives partly in water.

*Une **salamandre** est un genre de lézard qui vit en partie dans l'eau.*

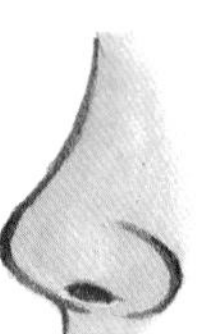

nose / *le nez*

We breathe and smell through our **nose**.

*Nous respirons et sentons avec notre **nez**.*

nurse / *l'infirmière*

A **nurse** looks after us when we are sick.

*Une **infirmière** s'occupe de nous lorsque nous sommes malades.*

nuts / *les noix*

When we have taken off the hard shells, we can eat **nuts**.

*Lorsque nous avons enlevé la coquille dure, nous pouvons manger les **noix**.*

oar / *la rame*

An **oar** is a long piece of wood with one flat end used to move a rowing boat.

*Une **rame** est un long morceau de bois, plat à un bout, utilisée pour faire avancer un bateau à **rames**.*

ocean / *l'océan*

An **ocean** is a very large sea. One **ocean** is the Atlantic **Ocean**.

*Un **océan** est une très grande mer. Un des **océans** s'appelle **l'océan** Atlantique.*

octopus / *la pieuvre*

An **octopus** lives in the sea. It has eight long legs with suckers on them.

*Une **pieuvre** vit dans la mer. Elle a huit longs bras couverts de ventouses.*

onion / *l'oignon*

Onions are good to eat. We cry when we cut an **onion**.

*Les **oignons** sont bons à manger. Nous pleurons lorsque nous coupons un **oignon**.*

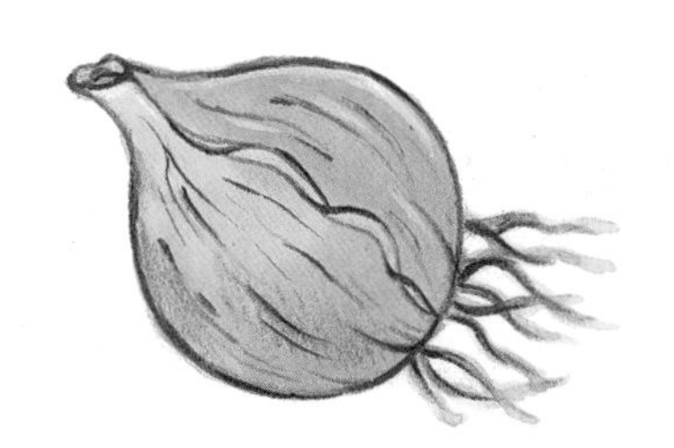

orange / *l'orange*

Orange is a colour. The boy's jumper is **orange**.

L'orange *est une couleur. Le chandail du garçon est* ***orange****.*

orange / *l'orange*

An **orange** is a kind of fruit. **Oranges** are sweet and good to eat.

Une ***orange*** *est une sorte de fruit. Les* ***oranges*** *sont sucrées et bonnes.*

orchard / *le verger*

A field full of fruit trees is called an **orchard**.

Un champ plein d'arbres fruitiers s'appelle un ***verger****.*

orchestra / *l'orchestre*

A lot of people making music together is called an **orchestra**.

Un groupe de personnes qui jouent de la musique ensemble s'appelle un ***orchestre****.*

ostrich / *l'autruche*

The **ostrich** is the largest bird in the world. An **ostrich** cannot fly.

***L'autruche** est le plus gros oiseau au monde. Une **autruche** ne peut pas voler.*

otter / *la loutre*

An **otter** is a brown, furry animal which swims well and eats fish.

*Une **loutre** est un animal à poils marron qui nage bien et mange du poisson.*

oven / *le four*

We cook lots of things like cakes and biscuits in an **oven**.

*On cuit beaucoup de choses, comme des gâteaux et des biscuits, au **four**.*

overalls / *la combinaison*

We wear **overalls** when working, to keep our clothes clean.

*Nous portons une **combinaison** pour travailler, pour ne pas salir nos vêtements.*

owl / *le hibou*

An **owl** is a bird with a big head and big eyes. **Owls** can see well in the dark.

*Un **hibou** est un oiseau avec une grosse tête et de gros yeux. Les **hiboux** voient bien dans le noir.*

Pp

pail / *le seau*

Jack and Jill carried a **pail** of water.

*Jacques et Jeanne ont porté un **seau** d'eau.*

paint / *la peinture*

We put **paint** on things to make them bright and pretty.

*Nous mettons de la **peinture** sur les objets pour les colorer et les rendre jolis.*

pancake / *la crêpe*

A **pancake** is flat and round, and good to eat.

*Une **crêpe** est plate et ronde, et délicieuse.*

panda / *le panda*

A **panda** is a big, black and white bear.

*Un **panda** est un gros ours noir et blanc.*

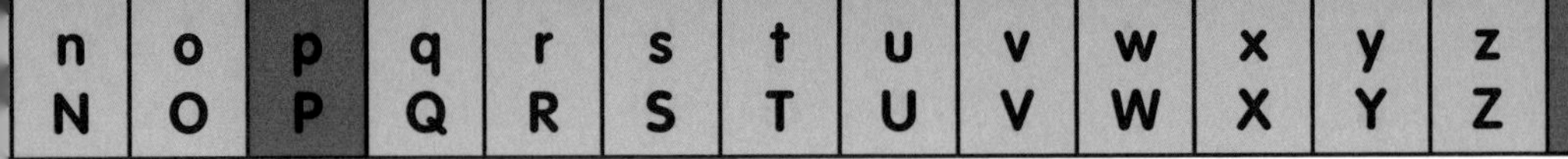

parade / *le défilé*

It is fun to watch a circus **parade**.

C'est amusant de regarder le ***défilé*** *d'un cirque.*

park / *le parc*

A **park** is a place with grass and trees, where anyone can play.

Un ***parc*** *est un endroit avec de l'herbe et des arbres où tout le monde peut jouer.*

parrot / *le perroquet*

A **parrot** is a colourful bird which can learn to say some words.

Un ***perroquet*** *est un oiseau aux plumes colorées qui peut apprendre à dire quelques mots.*

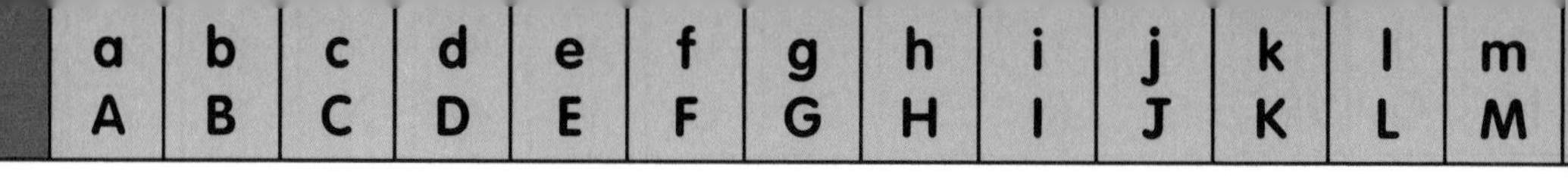

party / *la fête*

At a **party**, we have lots of fun. We have a **party** on our birthday.

*Durant une **fête**, on s'amuse beaucoup. Nous faisons la **fête** pour notre anniversaire.*

paw / *la patte*

A **paw** is an animal's foot with claws. Dogs and cats have **paws**.

*Une **patte** est le pied d'un animal. Les chiens et les chats ont des **pattes**.*

peacock / *le paon*

A **peacock** is a bird with a tail of colourful feathers.

*Un **paon** est un oiseau avec une queue au plumage coloré.*

pen / *le crayon / le stylo*

We can write and draw with a **pen**.

*Nous pouvons écrire et dessiner avec un **crayon** ou un **stylo**.*

pets / *les animaux de compagnie*

Pets are animals that we keep as special friends. A **pet** can be a dog, a cat, a rabbit, a canary or a goldfish.

Les ***animaux de compagnie*** *sont nos amis spéciaux. Un* ***animal de compagnie*** *peut être un chien, un chat, un lapin, un canari ou un poisson rouge.*

piano / *le piano*

We can make music with a **piano**.

Nous pouvons jouer de la musique avec un ***piano****.*

picnic / *le pique-nique*

When we eat outdoors, we are having a **picnic**.

Lorsque nous mangeons dehors, nous faisons un ***pique-nique****.*

pie / *la tarte*

A **pie** is filled with fruit or meat and cooked in the oven.

*Une **tarte** est garnie de fruits ou de viande et est cuite au four.*

pig / *le cochon*

A **pig** is a pink animal with a curly tail.

*Un **cochon** est un animal rose à la queue en tire-bouchon.*

pigeon / *le pigeon*

A **pigeon** is a bird which can find its way home from far away.

*Un **pigeon** est un oiseau qui peut retrouver le chemin de sa maison de très loin.*

pilot / *le pilote*

A **pilot** is the person who flies an aircraft.

*Le **pilote** est la personne qui **pilote** un avion.*

pink / *le rose*

Pink is a colour. The ballet shoes are **pink**.

*Le **rose** est une couleur. Les chaussons de danse sont **roses**.*

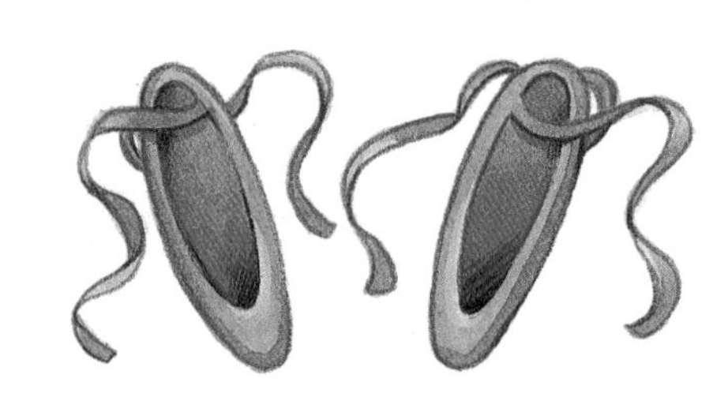

pirate / *le pirate*

A **pirate** is someone who robs from ships.

*Un **pirate** est une personne qui pille les navires.*

pocket / *la poche*

A **pocket** is like a little bag in our clothes where we can keep things.

*Une **poche** est un genre de petit sac dans nos vêtements où nous pouvons mettre des choses.*

polar bear / *l'ours polaire*

A **polar bear** is a wild animal that lives in very cold places.

*Un **ours polaire** est un animal sauvage qui vit dans des endroits très froids.*

pond / *la mare*

A **pond** is a small patch of water. Sometimes we have a **pond** in the garden.

*Une **mare** est une petite étendue d'eau. Parfois nous avons une **mare** dans le jardin.*

pony / *le poney*
A **pony** is a little horse.
*Un **poney** est un petit cheval.*

puppet / *la marionnette*
We play with a **puppet** by moving its strings. There are also glove **puppets**.
*Nous jouons avec une **marionnette** en faisant bouger ses fils. Il y a aussi des **marionnettes** à gaine.*

puppy / *le chiot*
A **puppy** is a young dog.
*Un **chiot** est un jeune chien.*

purple / *le violet*
Purple is a colour. The flowers are **purple**.
*Le **violet** est une couleur. Les fleurs sont **violettes**.*

purse / *le porte-monnaie*
We put money in a **purse** to keep it safe.
*Nous mettons l'argent dans un **porte-monnaie** pour ne pas le perdre.*

quack / *le couac*

Ducks **quack**. "**Quack**" is the sound they make.

*Les canards font **couac**. «**Couac**» est le son que font les canards.*

queen / *la reine*

A **queen** is the head of a country. The wife of a king is also a **queen**.

*Une **reine** est le chef d'un pays. La femme d'un roi s'appelle aussi une **reine**.*

quilt / *le duvet*

A **quilt** is the warm, padded cover on our bed.

*Le **duvet** est la couverture chaude et matelassée sur notre lit.*

quiver / *le carquois*

We carry arrows in a **quiver**.

*Nous portons des flèches dans un **carquois**.*

Rr

rabbit / *le lapin*

A **rabbit** is a small, furry animal, with very long ears.

*Un **lapin** est un petit animal à poils, avec de très longues oreilles.*

race / *la course*

We have a **race** to see who is the fastest at something. The children are in a swimming **race**.

*Nous faisons la **course** pour voir qui est le plus rapide. Les enfants font une **course** de natation.*

raft / *le radeau*

A **raft** is a flat boat made out of wood.

*Un **radeau** est un bateau plat en bois.*

railway / *le chemin de fer*

A **railway** is the rail track that trains and trams run on.

Le ***chemin de fer*** *est la voie sur laquelle les trains et les tramways roulent.*

rain / *la pluie*

Rain falls on us from the clouds. We get wet when it is **raining**.

La ***pluie*** *qui nous tombe dessus vient des nuages. Nous sommes mouillés lorsqu'il* ***pleut****.*

rainbow / *l'arc-en-ciel*

When the sun shines after it has rained, we sometimes see a **rainbow**.

Quand le soleil brille après la pluie, nous voyons parfois un ***arc-en-ciel****.*

rattle / *le hochet*

A baby will play with a **rattle**. A **rattle** makes a rattling noise.

Un bébé joue avec un ***hochet****. Un* ***hochet*** *fait des bruits secs.*

red / *le rouge*

Red is a colour. The bus is **red**.

*Le **rouge** est une couleur.*
*L'autobus est **rouge**.*

reindeer / *le renne*

A **reindeer** is an animal with very large horns.

*Un **renne** est un animal avec de très grands bois.*

ring / *la bague*

Sometimes we wear a **ring** on our finger. A **ring** is a circle.

*Parfois nous portons une **bague** au doigt. Une **bague** est un cercle.*

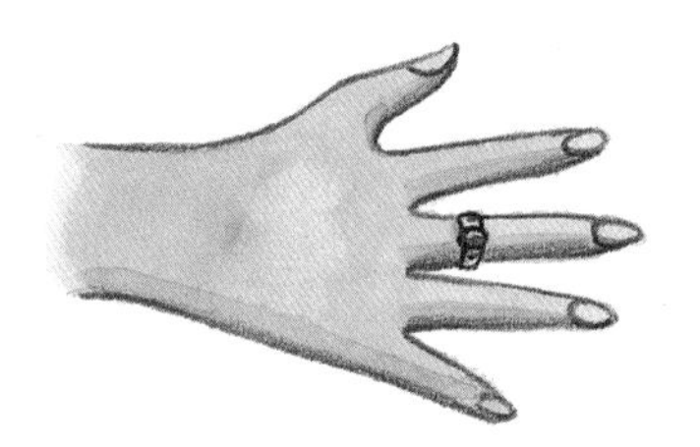

river / *la rivière*

A **river** is a large stream of moving water.

*Une **rivière** est un gros cours d'eau.*

robot / *le robot*

This toy **robot** is a machine in the shape of a person.

*Ce **robot**-jouet est une machine qui ressemble à une personne.*

rocket / *la fusée*

A **rocket** shoots up into the air. It is fun to see **rockets** when they are fireworks.

*Une **fusée** monte en chandelle. Il est amusant de regarder les **fusées** durant les feux d'artifice.*

rocking horse / *le cheval à bascule*

When we are little, we can play on a **rocking horse**.

*Lorsque nous sommes petits, nous pouvons jouer sur un **cheval à bascule**.*

roller skates / *les patins à roulettes*

We can move fast when we play on **roller skates**.

*Nous pouvons avancer vite lorsque nous faisons du **patin à roulettes**.*

root / *la racine*

A **root** is the part of a tree or plant under the ground.

*Une **racine** est la partie d'un arbre ou d'une plante qui est sous la terre.*

runway / *la piste*

Aircraft land and take off from a **runway**. A **runway** is a road for aircraft.

*Les avions atterrissent et décollent sur une **piste**. Une **piste** est une route pour avions.*

Ss

saddle / *la selle*

You sit in a **saddle** when you ride a horse.

*Tu t'assois sur une **selle** lorsque tu montes à cheval.*

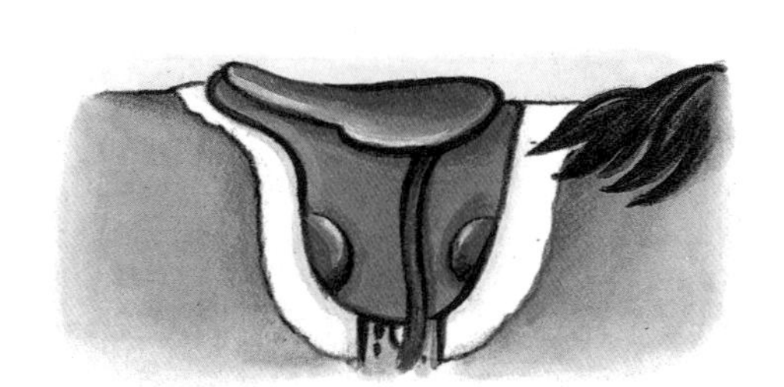

sail / *la voile*

The wind blows into the **sail** and moves the boat along.

*Le vent souffle sur la **voile** et fait avancer le bateau.*

salad / *la salade*

A **salad** is a mixture of vegetables or fruit. **Salads** are cold.

*Une **salade** est un mélange de légumes ou de fruits. Les **salades** sont froides.*

sandcastle / *le château de sable*

It is fun to build a **sandcastle** on the beach.

*C'est amusant de construire un **château de sable** à la plage.*

Santa Claus / *le Père Noël*

Santa Claus brings us presents at Christmas.

*Le **Père Noël** nous amène des cadeaux à Noël.*

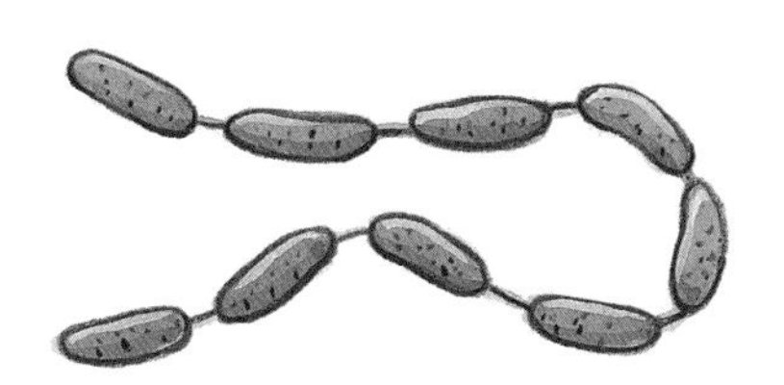

sausages / *les saucisses*

Here is a string of **sausages**. Most children enjoy eating **sausages**.

*Voici un chapelet de **saucisses**. La plupart des enfants aiment manger des **saucisses**.*

saw / *la scie*

A **saw** has a sharp, jagged edge. We cut things with a **saw**.

*Une **scie** a une lame tranchante et dentée. Nous coupons des choses avec une **scie**.*

school / *l'école*

People go to **school** to learn things. Children learn to read and write at **school**.

*On va à **l'école** pour apprendre. Les enfants apprennent à lire et à écrire à **l'école**.*

scissors / *les ciseaux*

Scissors will cut paper and cloth. We say that we have a pair of **scissors**.

*Les **ciseaux** coupent le papier et le tissu. On dit qu'on a une paire de **ciseaux**.*

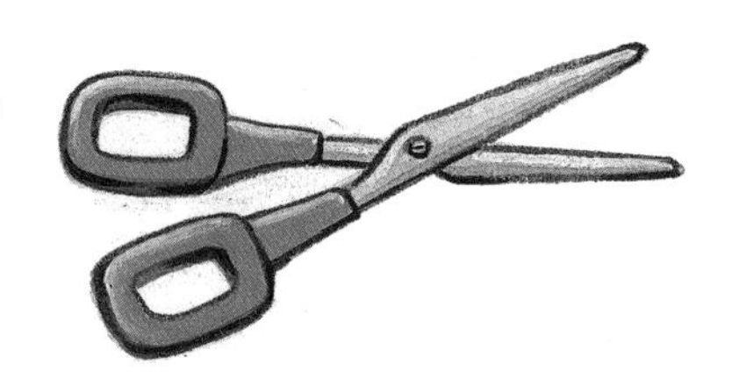

sea / *la mer*

The **sea** is the water that covers most of the earth. **Sea** water is salty.

*La **mer** est l'eau qui recouvre presque toute la terre. L'eau de **mer** est salée.*

seal / *le phoque*

A **seal** is an animal with fur and flippers which spends most of its time in the sea.

*Un **phoque** est un animal à poils et à nageoires qui passe la plupart de son temps dans la mer.*

seashell / *le coquillage*

We find **seashells** beside the sea. A little animal used to live in every **seashell**.

*Nous trouvons des **coquillages** à la plage. Un petit animal habitait dans chaque **coquillage**.*

see-saw / *la bascule*

The children are playing on the **see-saw**.

*Les enfants jouent à la **bascule**.*

shadow / *l'ombre*

A light in front of us makes a **shadow** behind us.

*Une lumière devant nous crée une **ombre** derrière nous.*

shark / *le requin*

A **shark** lives in the sea. Some **sharks** eat people!

*Le **requin** vit dans la mer. Certains **requins** mangent les gens!*

sheep / *le mouton*

We keep **sheep** on farms. Wool is made from a **sheep's** coat.

*On élève les **moutons** à la ferme. La laine provient de la toison du **mouton**.*

ship / *le navire*

We travel across the sea in a **ship**. Some **ships** are very big.

*Nous voyageons en mer sur un **navire**. Certains **navires** sont très grands.*

shop / *le magasin*

We can buy things in a **shop**.

*Nous pouvons acheter des choses dans un **magasin**.*

shower / *la douche*

A **shower** sprays us with water so that we can wash ourselves.

*Une **douche** nous arrose d'eau, pour que nous puissions nous laver.*

signpost / *le panneau*

A **signpost** points the way to somewhere.

*Un **panneau** indique comment se rendre quelque part.*

singer / *le chanteur / la chanteuse*

Someone who makes music with their voice is a **singer**.

*Quelqu'un qui fait de la musique avec sa voix s'appelle un **chanteur** ou une **chanteuse**.*

skateboard / *la planche à roulettes*

A **skateboard** is a board with wheels which you can play on.

*Une **planche à roulettes** est une planche munie de roulettes sur laquelle tu peux jouer.*

skeleton / *le squelette*

Our **skeleton** is made up of all the bones in our body.

*Notre **squelette** est fait de tous les os de notre corps.*

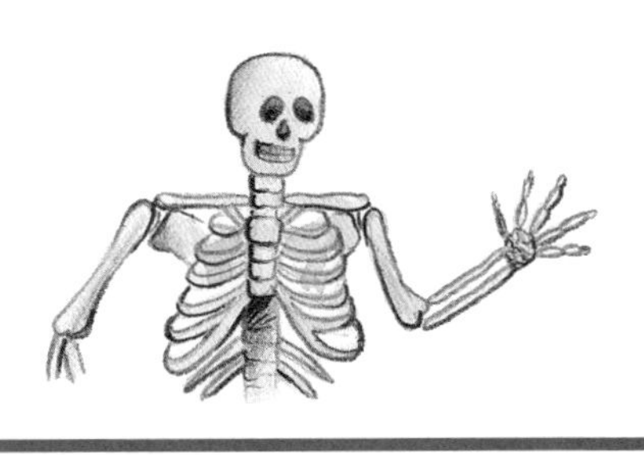

sleep / *dormir*

We go to bed to **sleep**. When we are tired, we need to have a **sleep**.

*Nous allons au lit pour **dormir**. Quand nous sommes fatigués, nous avons besoin de **dormir**.*

sleigh / *le traîneau*

We travel over the snow in a **sleigh**. Santa uses a **sleigh**.

*Nous voyageons sur la neige en **traîneau**. Le Père Noël utilise un **traîneau**.*

smoke / *la fumée*

Smoke is the dark cloud that we see when something is burning.

*La **fumée** est le nuage sombre que nous voyons lorsque quelque chose brûle.*

snail / *l'escargot*

A **snail** is a small animal with a shell on its back which moves very slowly.

*Un **escargot** est un petit animal qui a une coquille sur le dos et qui se déplace très lentement.*

snakes / *les serpents*

Snakes are long, thin animals without legs. A **snake** slides along the ground.

*Les **serpents** sont des animaux longs et minces sans pattes. Un **serpent** se déplace en glissant par terre.*

snow / *la neige*

When it is cold, flakes of frozen water called **snow** fall from the sky.

Quand il fait froid, des flocons d'eau gelée, que l'on appelle ***neige****, tombent du ciel.*

spider / *l'araignée*

A **spider** is a small animal with eight legs which makes a web to catch its food.

Une ***araignée*** *est un petit animal à huit pattes qui tisse des toiles pour attraper à manger.*

squirrel / *l'écureuil*

A **squirrel** is a red or grey animal with a bushy tail. **Squirrels** live in trees.

Un ***écureuil*** *est un animal roux ou gris à queue touffue. Les* ***écureuils*** *vivent dans les arbres.*

stars / *les étoiles*

We see tiny lights in the sky at night. They are the **stars**.

Nous voyons de toutes petites lumières dans le ciel la nuit. Ce sont les ***étoiles****.*

starfish / *l'étoile de mer*

A **starfish** is a star-shaped fish.

*Une **étoile de mer** est un poisson en forme d'étoile.*

steeple / *le clocher*

A **steeple** is the high, pointed top of a church.

*Le **clocher** est le sommet pointu d'une église.*

storm / *la tempête*

It is a **storm** when there are strong winds and heavy rain.

*Il y a une **tempête** quand le vent souffle fort et qu'il pleut très fort.*

street / *la rue*

A road with houses or shops along it is a **street**.

*Une route longée de maisons ou de magasins s'appelle une **rue**.*

submarine / *le sous-marin*

A **submarine** is a boat that can go under the water.

*Un **sous-marin** est un bateau qui peut aller sous l'eau.*

sunflower / *le tournesol*

A **sunflower** is a large, golden flower which always faces the sun.

*Un **tournesol** est une grosse fleur dorée qui se tourne toujours vers le soleil.*

supermarket / le *supermarché*

A very big shop is called a **supermarket**.

*Un très grand magasin s'appelle un **supermarché**.*

swan / *le cygne*

A **swan** is a big, white bird with a very long neck.

*Un **cygne** est un grand oiseau blanc avec un très long cou.*

Tt

tail / *la queue*

A **tail** is the end of something. Most animals have **tails**.

*La **queue** est la fin de quelque chose. La plupart des animaux ont une **queue**.*

tambourine / *le tambourin*

Sometimes we make music with a **tambourine**.

*Quelquefois nous jouons de la musique avec un **tambourin**.*

tangle / *emmêler*

The dogs' leads are in a **tangle**. They are all knotted together.

*Les laisses des chiens sont **emmêlées**. Elles sont tout embrouillées.*

taxi / *le taxi*

A **taxi** is like a car that will take us places for money.

*Un **taxi** est une voiture qui nous emmènera quelque part pour de l'argent.*

teacher / le *maître d'école* / *la maîtresse d'école*

The **teacher** teaches us things at school.

*La **maîtresse d'école** nous apprend des choses à l'école.*

Teddy bear / *l'ours en peluche*

A **Teddy bear** is soft and warm.

*Un **ours en peluche** est doux et chaud.*

telephone / *le téléphone*

We talk on the **telephone** to someone far away.

*Nous parlons au **téléphone** à quelqu'un qui est loin.*

television / *la télévision*

Television shows us pictures in our homes from far away.

*La **télévision** nous montre chez nous des images de très loin.*

tent / *la tente*

When we are camping, we sleep in a **tent**.

*Quand nous campons, nous dormons sous une **tente**.*

theatre / *le théâtre*

We go to the **theatre** to see actors and hear music.

*Nous allons au **théâtre** pour regarder des acteurs et écouter de la musique.*

thermometer / *le thermomètre*

When we are not well, a **thermometer** measures how hot we are.

*Quand nous ne sommes pas bien, un **thermomètre** mesure notre température.*

thumb / *le pouce*

On each hand, we have a **thumb** and four other fingers.

*A chaque main, nous avons un **pouce** et quatre autres doigts.*

tiger / *le tigre*

A **tiger** is a big, wild animal with a striped coat.

*Un **tigre** est un grand animal sauvage à la fourrure rayée.*

toes / *les orteils*

We have five **toes** on the end of each foot.

*Nous avons cinq **orteils** au bout de chaque pied.*

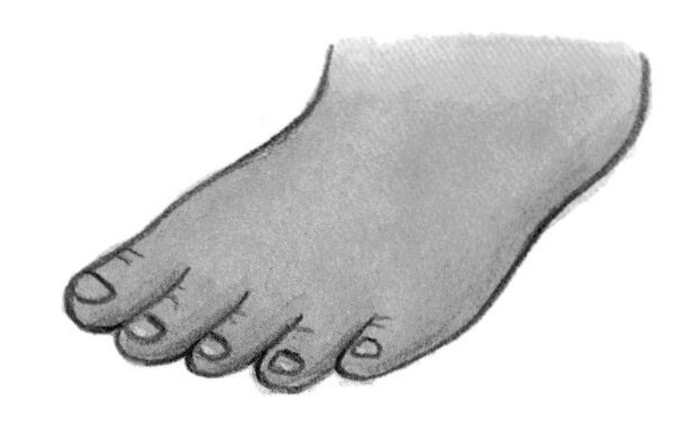

tomato / *la tomate*

A **tomato** is a soft red fruit. We eat **tomatoes** raw or cooked.

*La **tomate** est un fruit rouge et mou. Nous mangeons les **tomates** crues ou cuites.*

tools / *les outils*

Tools help us to do work.
A screwdriver is a **tool**.

*Les **outils** nous aident à faire notre travail. Un tournevis est un **outil**.*

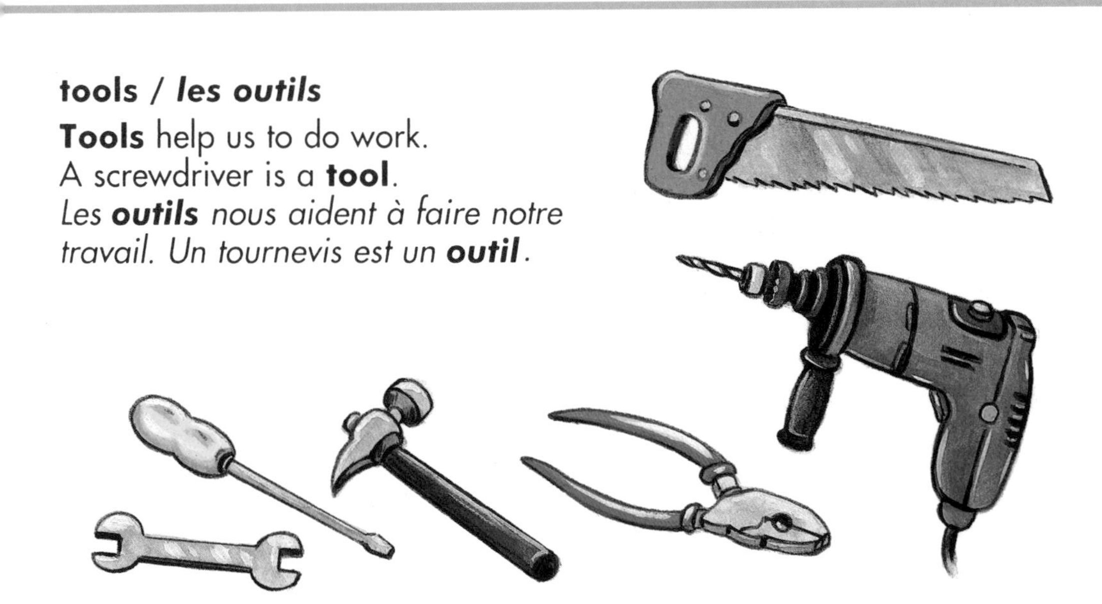

tooth / *la dent*

A **tooth** is one of the hard white bones in our mouth. We bite things with our **teeth**.

*Une **dent** est un des os blancs et durs dans notre bouche. Nous mordons les choses avec nos **dents**.*

tortoise / *la tortue*

A **tortoise** is a slow-moving animal with a hard shell on its back.

*Une **tortue** est un animal lent avec une carapace sur le dos.*

tower / *la tour*

The walls of a castle have **towers** at each corner. A **tower** is a tall, narrow building.

*Les murs d'un château ont des **tours** à chaque coin. Une **tour** est un bâtiment haut et étroit.*

toys / *les jouets*

Toy boats and **toy** drums are **toys**.

*Les bateaux miniatures et les tambours d'enfant sont des **jouets**.*

tractor / *le tracteur*

A **tractor** can pull heavy things over muddy ground.

*Un **tracteur** peut remorquer des choses lourdes en terrain boueux.*

train / *le train*

A **train** is pulled by a locomotive. Sometimes there are lots of wagons in a **train**.

*Un **train** est tiré par une locomotive. Quelquefois un **train** a beaucoup de wagons.*

tree / *l'arbre*

A **tree** is a very big plant. **Trees** have branches and leaves.

*Un **arbre** est une très grande plante. Les **arbres** ont des branches et des feuilles.*

truck / *le camion*

Lots of things are carried by road in a **truck**.

*Beaucoup de choses sont transportées en **camion** par la route.*

trumpet / *la trompette*

We can make music by blowing a **trumpet**.

*On peut faire de la musique en soufflant dans une **trompette**.*

tunnel / *le tunnel*

A **tunnel** is a passage under the ground.

*Un **tunnel** est un passage sous terre.*

Uu

umbrella / *le parapluie*

An **umbrella** will keep us dry when it rains.

*Un **parapluie** nous gardera au sec quand il pleut.*

unicorn / *la licorne*

In fairy tales, a **unicorn** is a magic animal with one horn on its head.

*Dans les contes de fées, une **licorne** est un animal magique avec une corne sur la tête.*

uniform / *l'uniforme*

A **uniform** is a set of special clothes that some people wear. A nurse wears a **uniform**.

*Un **uniforme** est un ensemble de vêtements spéciaux que certaines personnes portent. Une infirmière porte un **uniforme**.*

vacuum cleaner / *l'aspirateur*
A **vacuum cleaner** is a machine that sucks up dirt.
*Un **aspirateur** est une machine qui aspire la saleté.*

valley / *la vallée*
A **valley** is the low piece of land between hills.
*Une **vallée** est la partie basse entre les collines.*

van / *la camionnette*
A small truck for delivering things is called a **van**.
*Un petit camion de livraison s'appelle une **camionnette**.*

vase / *le vase*
We put flowers in a **vase**.
*Nous mettons des fleurs dans un **vase**.*

vegetables / *les légumes*

Vegetables are plants that we grow for food. **Vegetables** are good for us.

*Les **légumes** sont des plantes que nous faisons pousser pour nous nourrir. Les **légumes** sont bons pour la santé.*

violin / *le violon*

We can make music on a **violin** by rubbing the bow against the strings.

*Nous pouvons jouer de la musique au **violon** en frottant l'archet sur les cordes.*

voice / *la voix*

When we sing and speak, we are using our **voice**.

*Lorsque nous chantons et parlons, nous utilisons notre **voix**.*

wagon / *le wagon*

A **wagon** is a cart for carrying heavy loads. Sometimes a **wagon** is pulled by horses.

*Un **wagon** est un chariot utilisé pour transporter des choses lourdes. Quelquefois un **wagon** est tiré par des chevaux.*

waist / *la taille*

Our **waist** is in the middle of our body. Our body bends at the **waist**.

*Notre **taille** se trouve au milieu de notre corps. Notre corps se plie à la **taille**.*

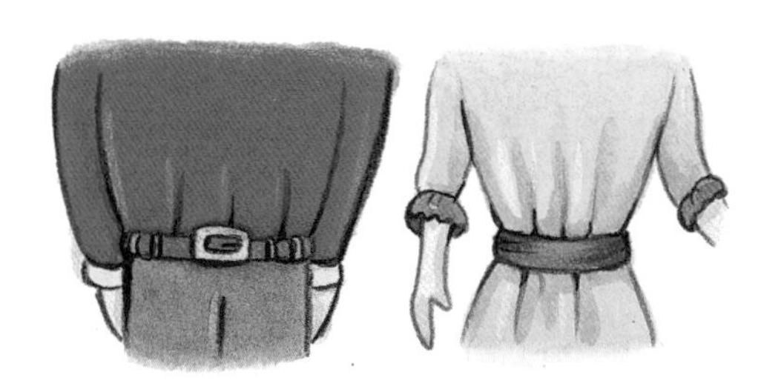

walrus / *le morse*

A **walrus** is a big sea animal with two long tusks.

*Un **morse** est un grand animal de mer avec deux longues défenses.*

watch / *la montre*

A **watch** is like a small clock that we wear on our arm.

*Une **montre** ressemble à une petite horloge que nous portons au bras.*

waterfall / *la cascade*

A stream of water falling over a cliff is called a **waterfall**.

*Un cours d'eau qui tombe d'une falaise s'appelle une **cascade**.*

well / *le puits*

A **well** is a deep hole in the ground with water in it.

*Un **puits** est un trou profond dans la terre avec de l'eau au fond.*

whale / *la baleine*

A **whale** is a big animal that lives in the sea.

*Une **baleine** est un gros animal qui vit dans la mer.*

wheelbarrow / *la brouette*

We use a **wheelbarrow** in the garden. A **wheelbarrow** has two handles and one wheel.

*Nous utilisons une **brouette** dans le jardin. Une **brouette** a deux manches et une roue.*

wigwam / *le wigwam*

A **wigwam** is a kind of tent that some American Indians used to live in.

*Un **wigwam** est un genre de tente dans laquelle certains Amérindiens habitaient.*

windmill / *le moulin à vent*

The wind blows round the sails of the **windmill**. **Windmills** are machines that can lift water.

*Le vent fait tourner les ailes du **moulin à vent**. Les **moulins à vent** sont des machines qui peuvent puiser de l'eau.*

wing / *l'aile*

The **wing** is the part of a bird that it uses to fly. Birds have two **wings**.

*L'**aile** est la partie que l'oiseau utilise pour voler. Les oiseaux ont deux **ailes**.*

woodpecker / *le pivert*

A **woodpecker** is a bird that pecks wood. You can often hear a **woodpecker** tapping on a tree.

*Un **pivert** est un oiseau qui frappe sur le bois. Tu peux souvent entendre un **pivert** frapper sur un arbre.*

worm / *le ver*

A **worm** is like a little snake that lives in the earth.

*Un **ver** ressemble à un petit serpent qui vit sous terre.*

wrist / *le poignet*

Our **wrist** joins our hand to our arm. We have two wrists.

*Notre **poignet** relie notre main à notre bras. Nous avons deux poignets.*

Xx

X-ray / *les rayons x*

A picture of the inside of our body is called an **x-ray**.

*L'image de l'intérieur de notre corps s'appelle une radio à **rayons x**.*

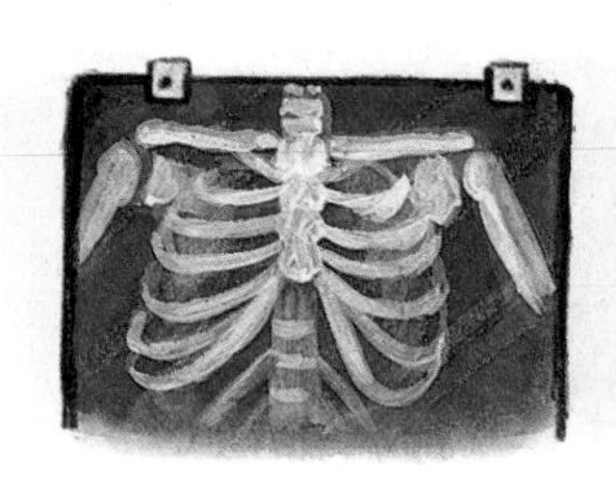

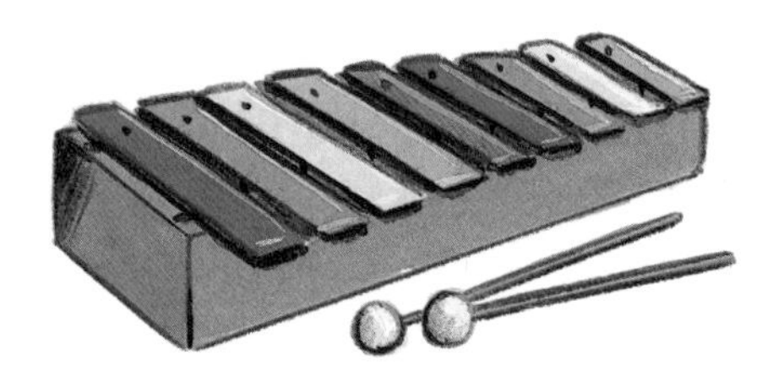

xylophone / *le xylophone*

We play a **xylophone** to make music.

*Nous jouons au **xylophone** pour faire de la musique.*

yacht / *le yacht*

A boat with large sails is called a **yacht**.

*Un bateau à grandes voiles s'appelle un **yacht**.*

yawn / *bailler*

We **yawn** when we are tired.

*Nous **baillons** quand nous sommes fatigués.*

yellow / *le jaune*

Yellow is a colour. The little bird is **yellow**.

*Le **jaune** est une couleur. Le petit oiseau est **jaune**.*

yo-yo / *le yo-yo*

A **yo-yo** is a toy. We spin a **yo-yo** up and down.

*Un **yo-yo** est un jouet. Nous faisons monter et descendre un **yo-yo**.*

Zz

zebra / *le zèbre*

A **zebra** is a wild animal like a striped horse.

*Un **zèbre** est un animal sauvage qui ressemble à un cheval rayé.*

zip / *la fermeture éclair*

A **zip** at the front of our jacket fastens the sides together.

*Une **fermeture éclair** sur le devant de notre veste attache les côtés ensemble.*

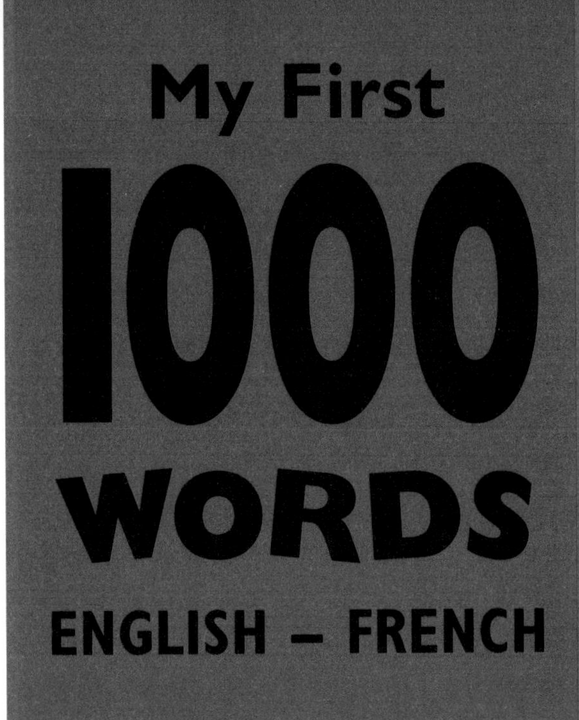

My First 1000 WORDS

ENGLISH – FRENCH

alarm clock
le réveil

butterfly
le papillon

parrot
le perroquet

rocket
la fusée

tractor
le tracteur

flower
la fleur

mother
la mère

father
le père

brother
le frère

sister
la sœur

contents: table des matières

la famille | the family

our bodies

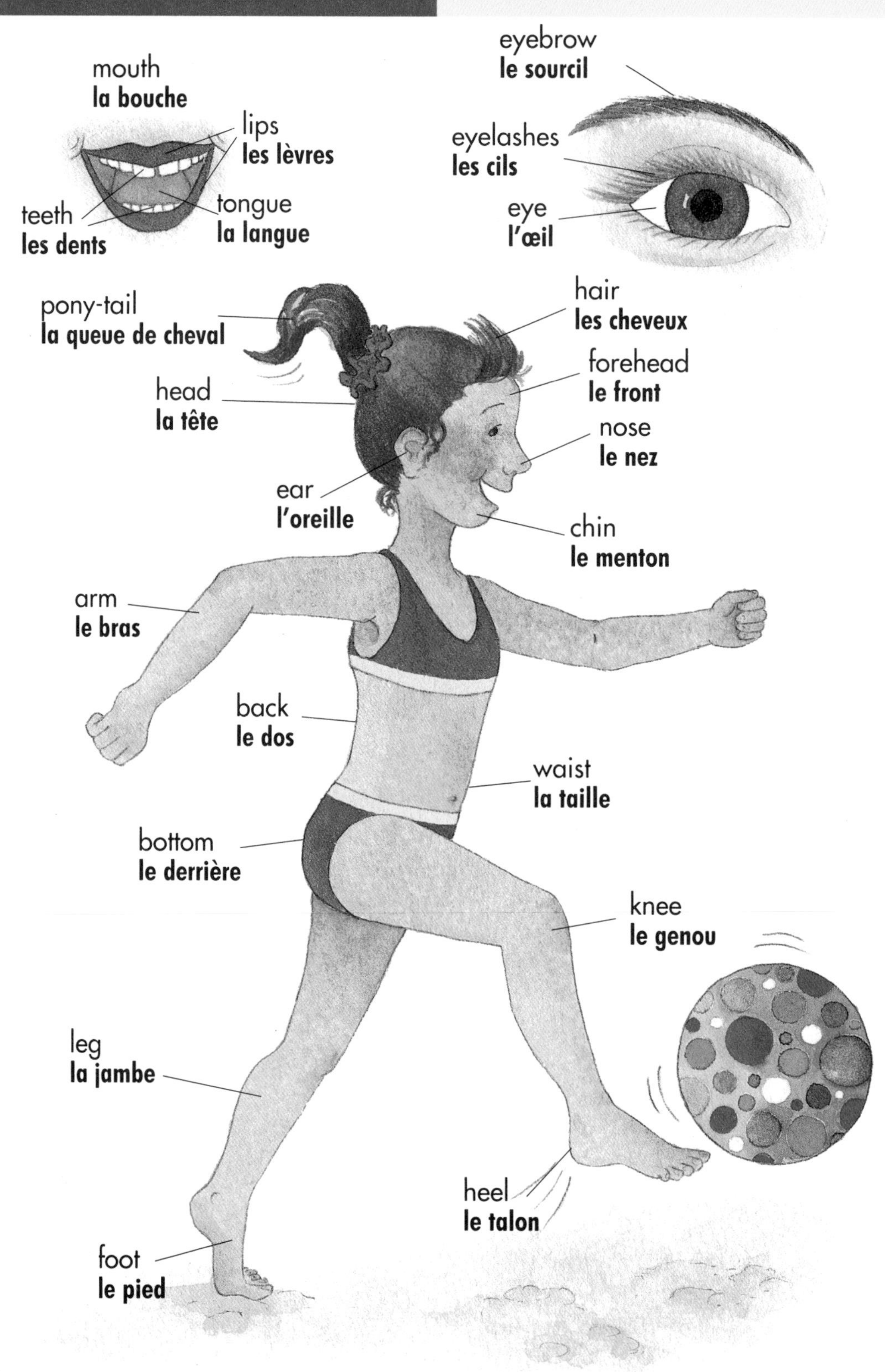

mouth
la bouche
lips
les lèvres
teeth
les dents
tongue
la langue
eyebrow
le sourcil
eyelashes
les cils
eye
l'œil
pony-tail
la queue de cheval
hair
les cheveux
forehead
le front
head
la tête
nose
le nez
ear
l'oreille
chin
le menton
arm
le bras
back
le dos
waist
la taille
bottom
le derrière
knee
le genou
leg
la jambe
heel
le talon
foot
le pied

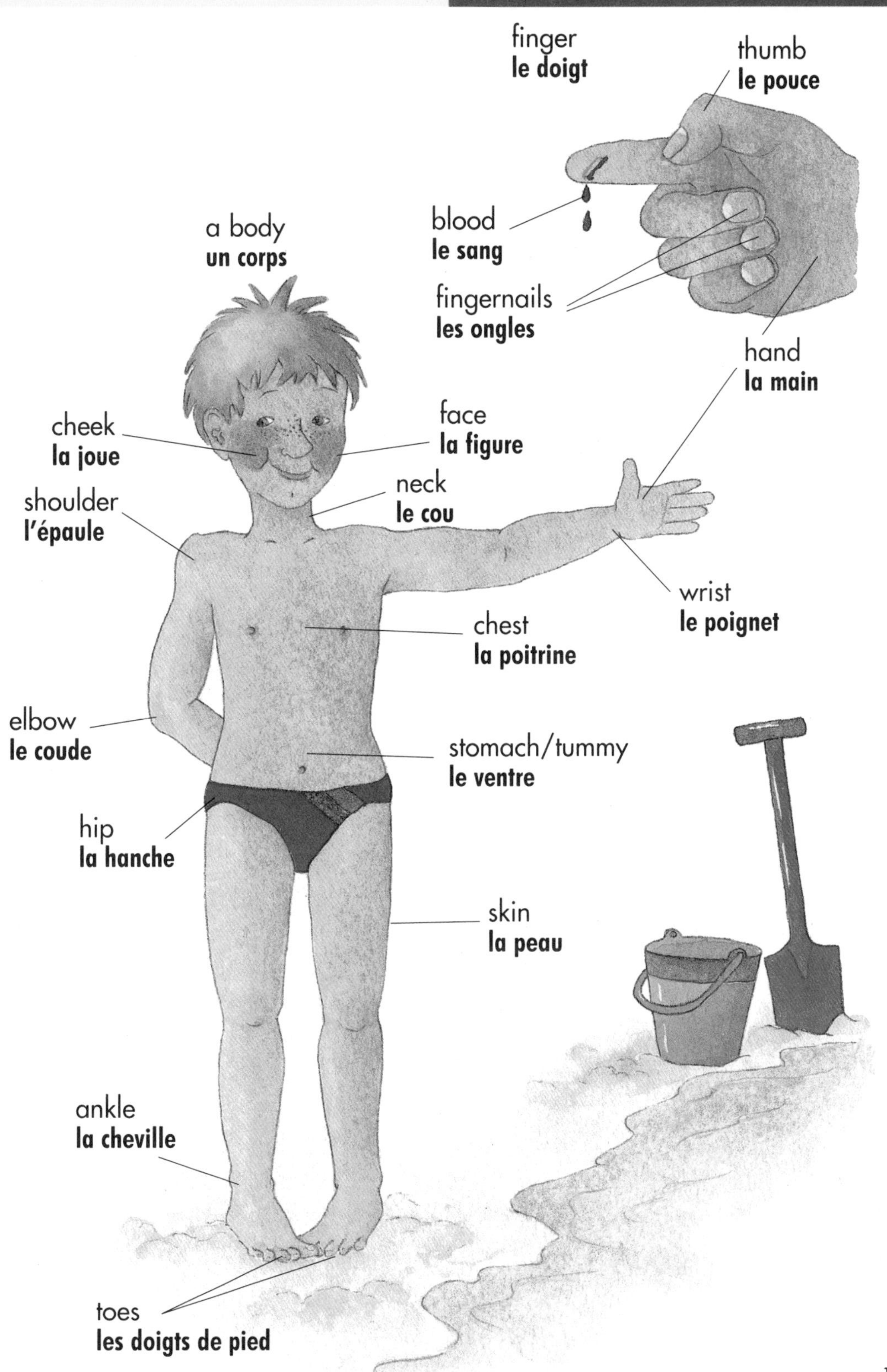
finger
le doigt
thumb
le pouce
blood
le sang
fingernails
les ongles
hand
la main
a body
un corps
cheek
la joue
face
la figure
neck
le cou
shoulder
l'épaule
wrist
le poignet
chest
la poitrine
elbow
le coude
stomach/tummy
le ventre
hip
la hanche
skin
la peau
ankle
la cheville
toes
les doigts de pied

more words

bald
chauve
man
l'homme
boy
le garçon
people
les gens
parents
les parents
moustache
la moustache
beard
la barbe
bride
la mariée
hear
entendre
taste
goûter
twins
les jumelles
bridegroom
le marié

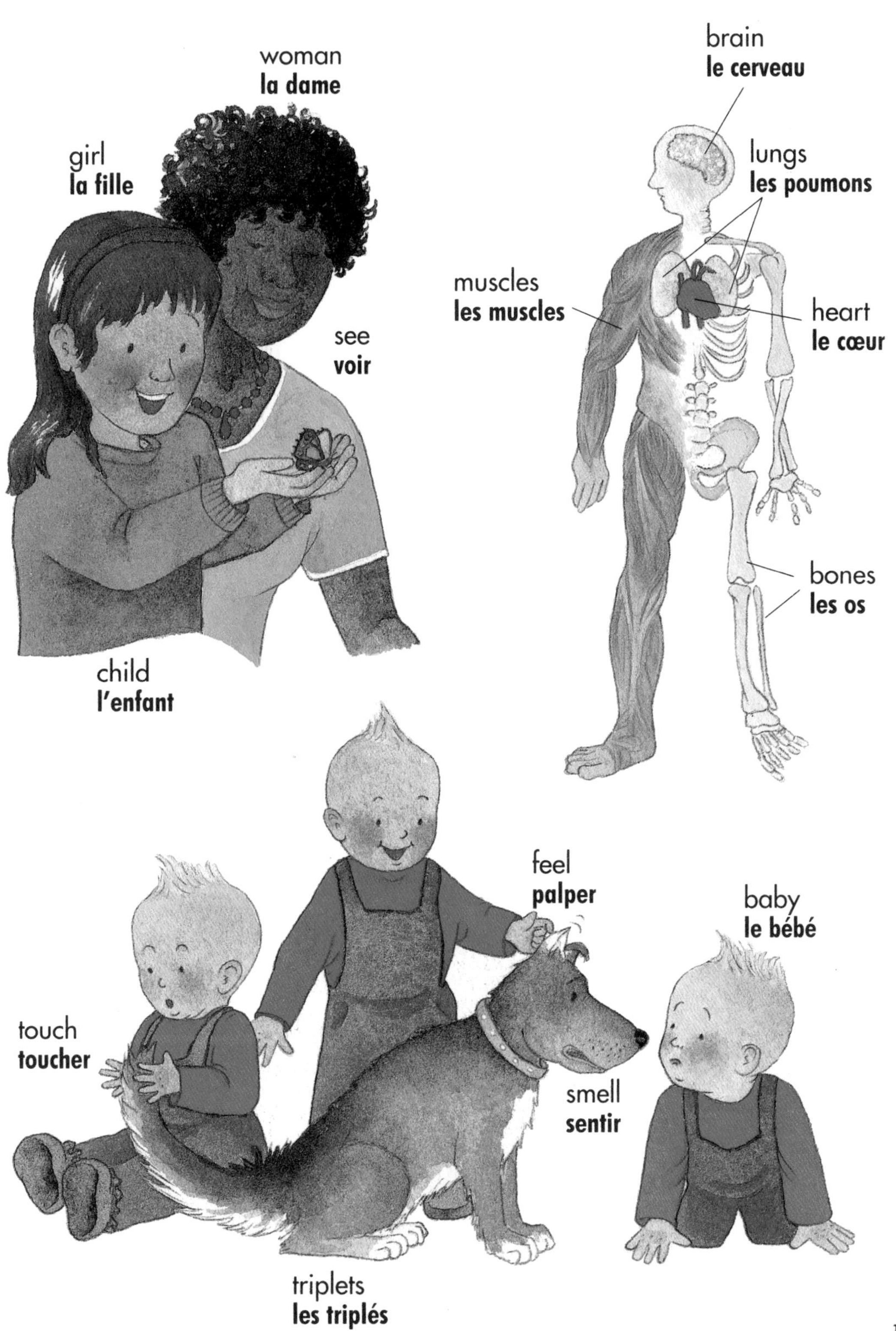
woman
la dame
girl
la fille
see
voir
child
l'enfant
brain
le cerveau
lungs
les poumons
muscles
les muscles
heart
le cœur
bones
les os
feel
palper
baby
le bébé
touch
toucher
smell
sentir
triplets
les triplés

clothes

dress
la robe

jumper
le pull

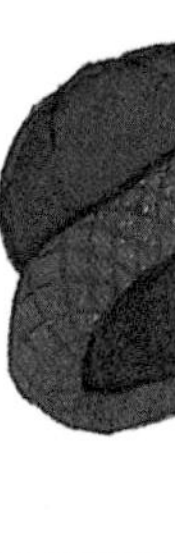

hat
le chapeau

knickers
la culotte

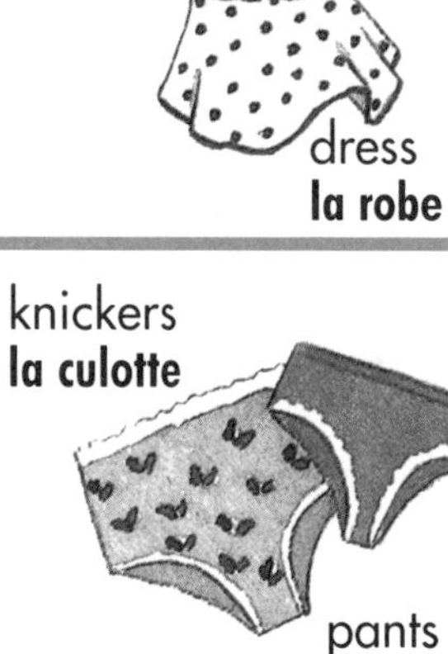

pants
le slip

dressing gown
la robe de chambre

trousers
le pantalon

anorak
l'anorak

socks
les chaussettes

blouse
le chemisier

skirt
la jupe

pyjamas
le pyjama

petticoat
le jupon

leggings
le caleçon

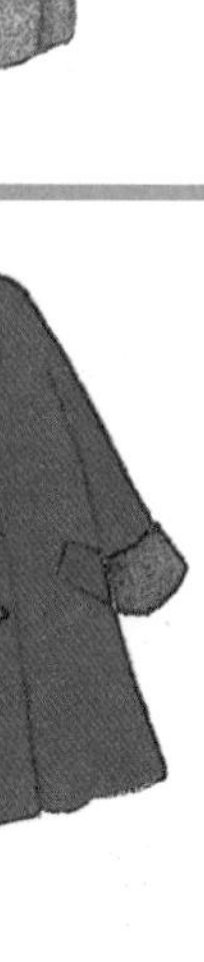

coat
le manteau

cap
la casquette

les vêtements

shorts
le short

raincoat
l'Imperméable

T-shirt
le tee-shirt

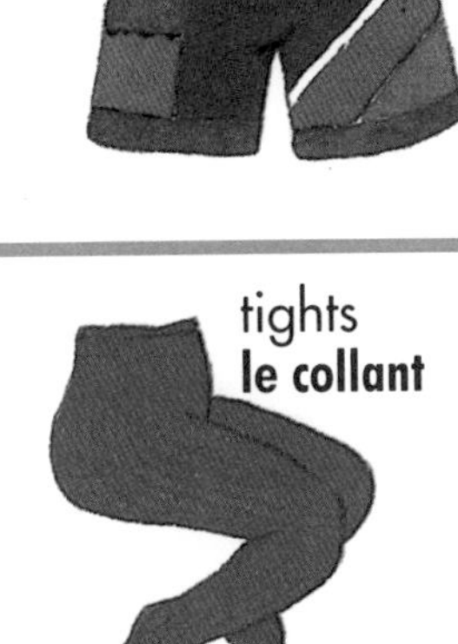

tights
le collant

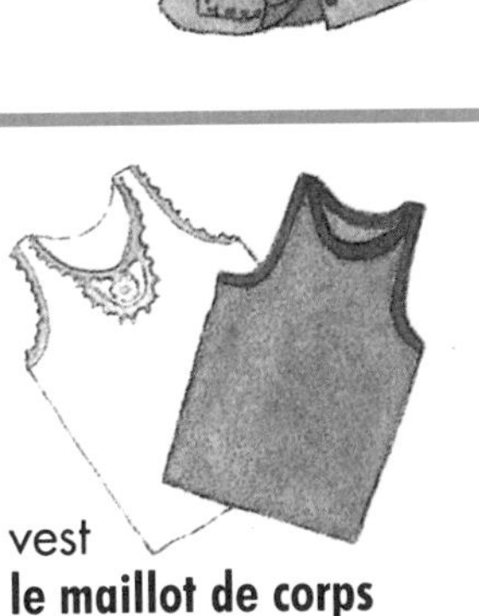

vest
le maillot de corps

jacket
la veste

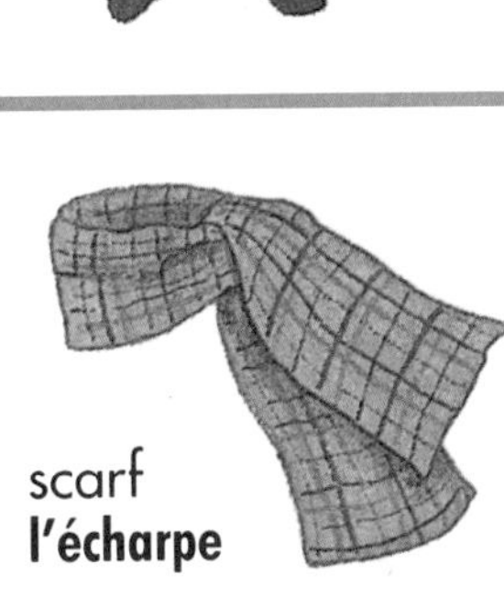

scarf
l'écharpe

nightdress
la chemise de nuit

jeans
le jean

underpants
le slip

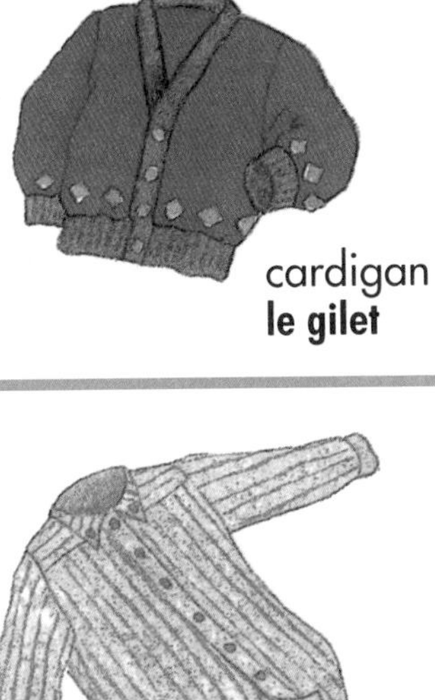

cardigan
le gilet

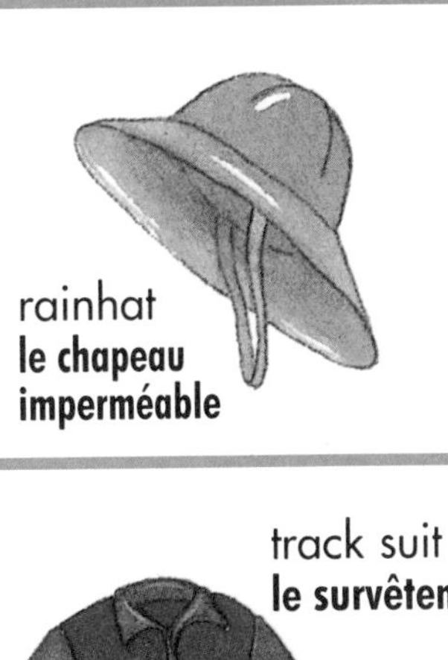

rainhat
le chapeau imperméable

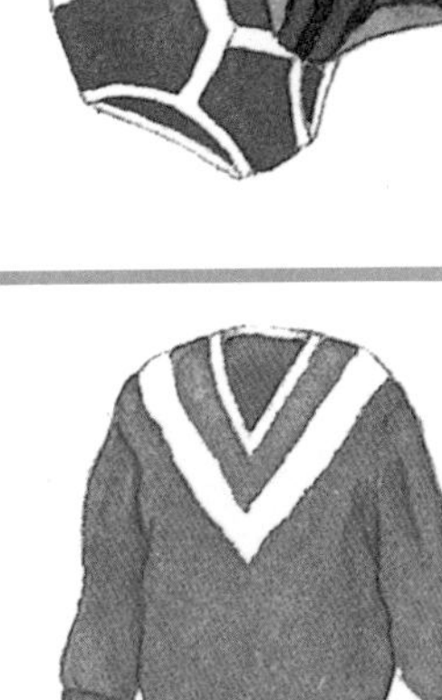

sweater
le pull

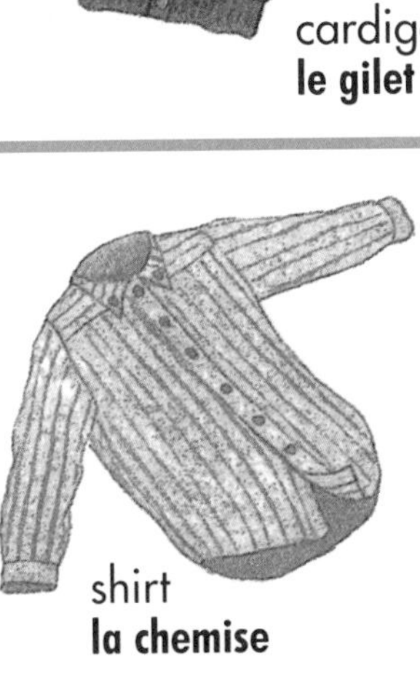

shirt
la chemise

track suit
le survêtement

more things to wear

laces
les lacets

slippers
les pantoufles

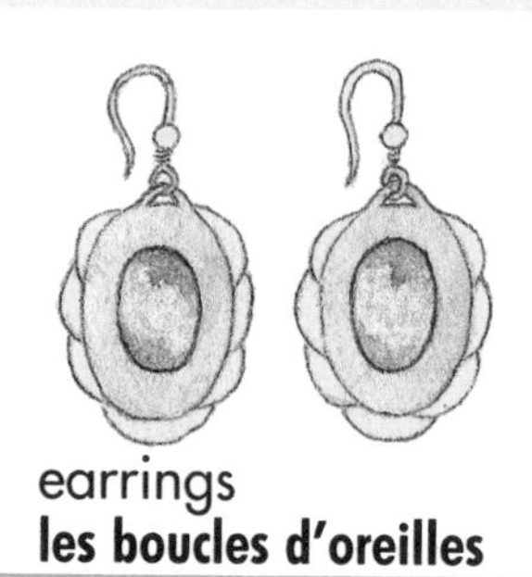

earrings
les boucles d'oreilles

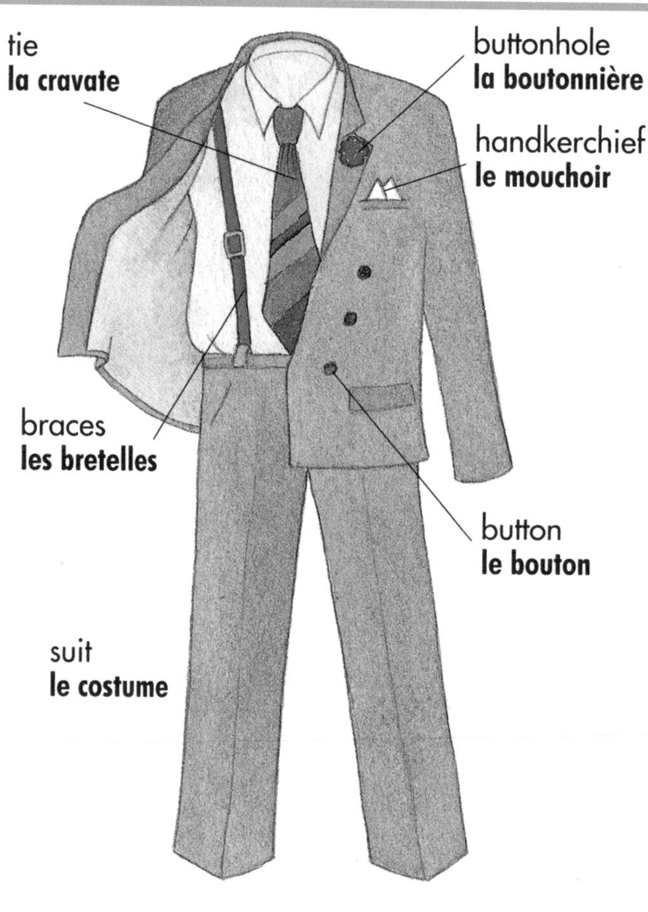

necklace
le collier

rubber boots
les bottes en caoutchouc

glasses
les lunettes

shoes
les chaussures

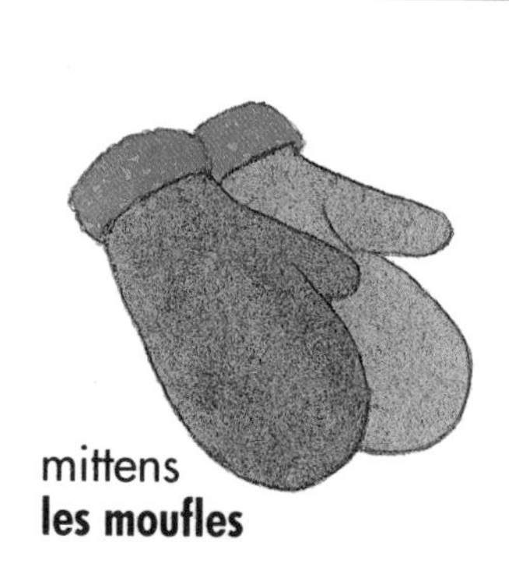

mittens
les moufles

apron
le tablier

d'autres choses à porter

overalls
le bleu

boots
les bottes

gloves
les gants

ring
la bague

trainers
les tennis

belt
la ceinture

buckle
la boucle

tiara
le diadème

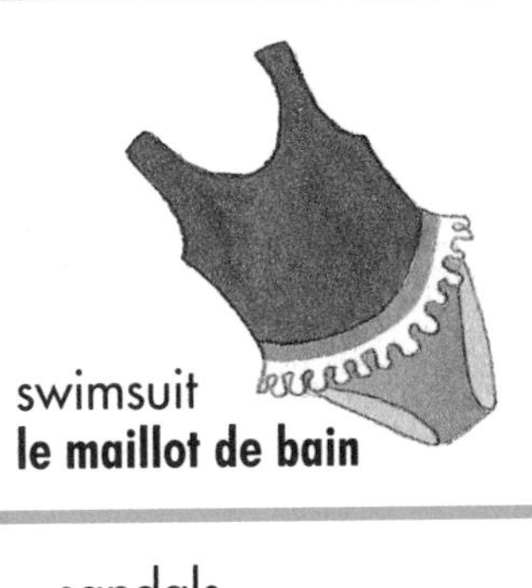

swimsuit
le maillot de bain

ribbon
le ruban

hairband
le bandeau

bracelet
le bracelet

brooch
la broche

sandals
les sandales

trunks
le caleçon de bain

the bedroom

bedside table
la table de nuit

lamp
la lampe

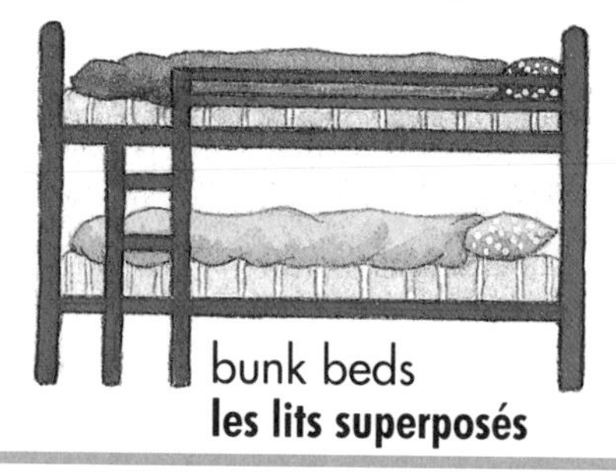

bunk beds
les lits superposés

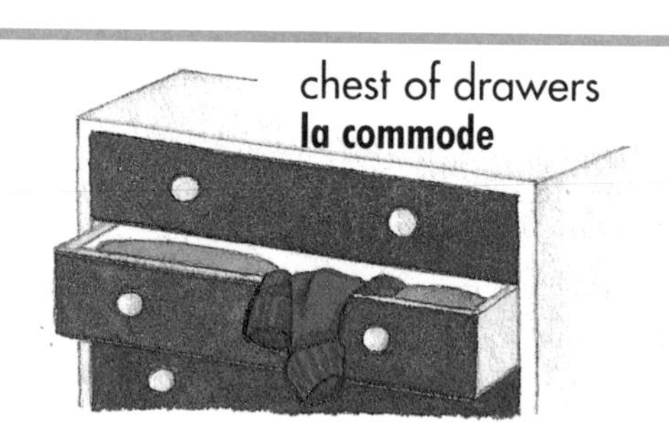

chest of drawers
la commode

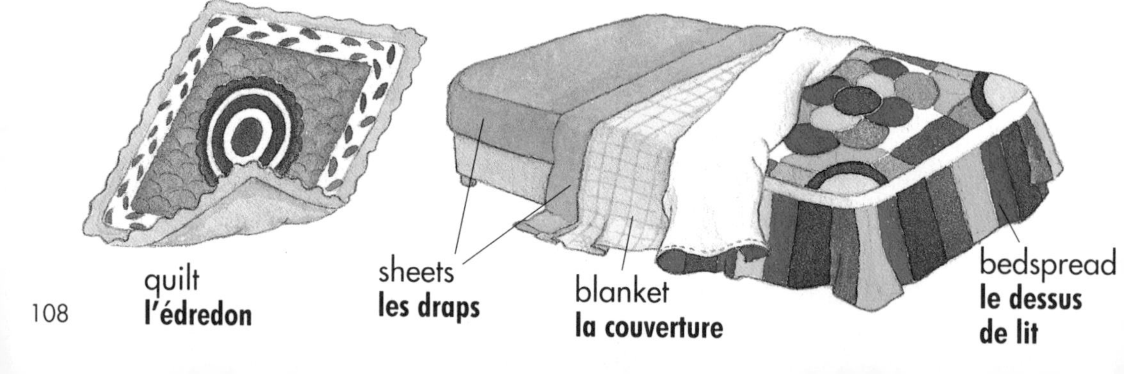

quilt
l'édredon

sheets
les draps

blanket
la couverture

bedspread
le dessus de lit

la chambre

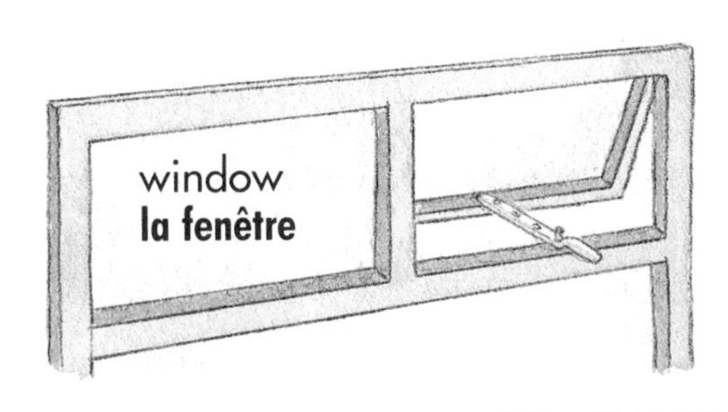
window
la fenêtre

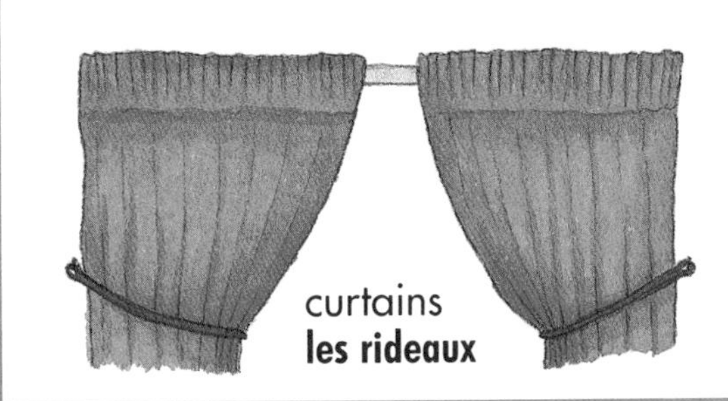
curtains
les rideaux

alarm clock
le réveil

wardrobe
l'armoire

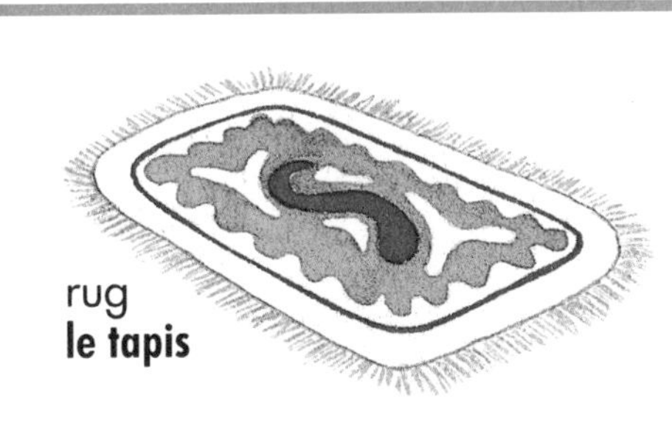
rug
le tapis

bed
le lit

cot
le lit d'enfant

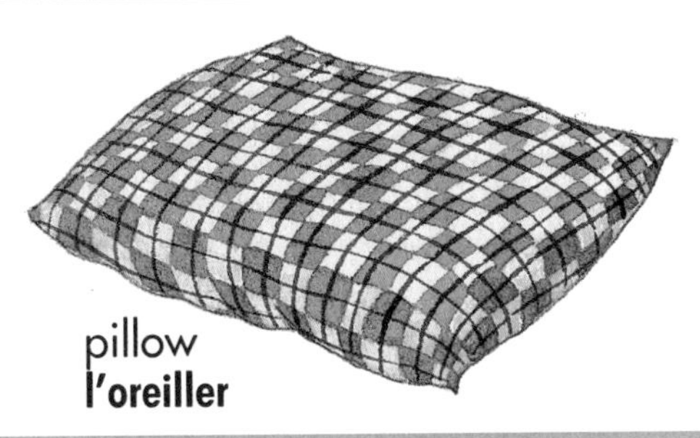
pillow
l'oreiller

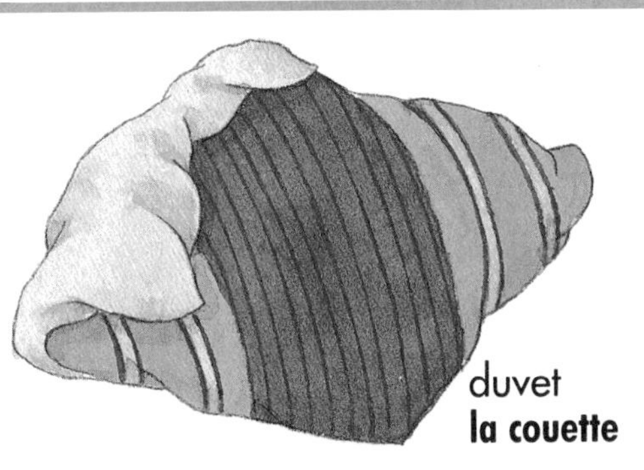
duvet
la couette

cradle
le berceau

the bathroom

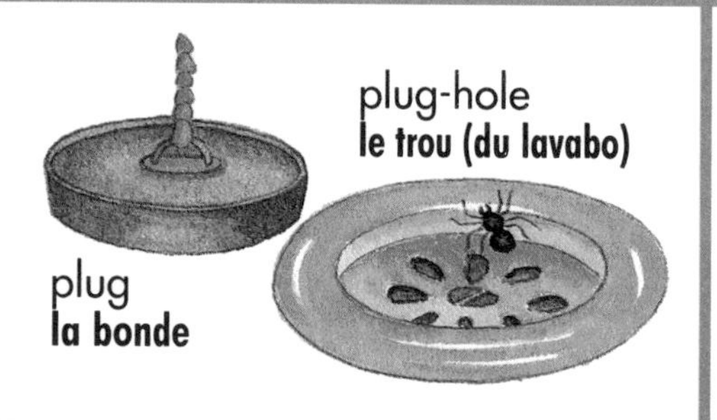

plug-hole
le trou (du lavabo)

plug
la bonde

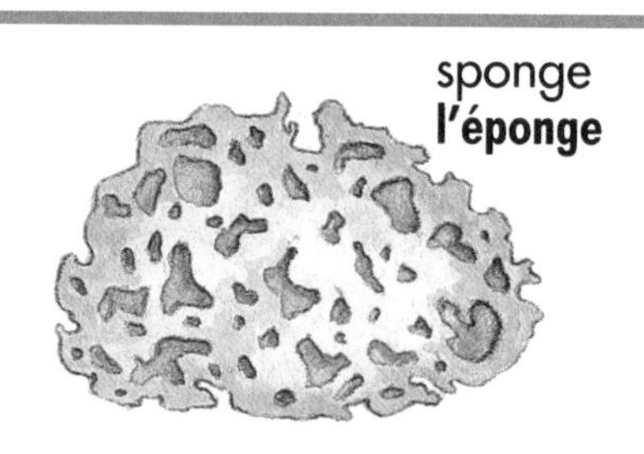

sponge
l'éponge

bath
la baignoire

bubbles
les bulles

toilet
les toilettes

toilet paper
le papier hygiénique

la salle de bain

wash-basin
le lavabo

towel
la serviette

shower-curtain
le rideau de douche

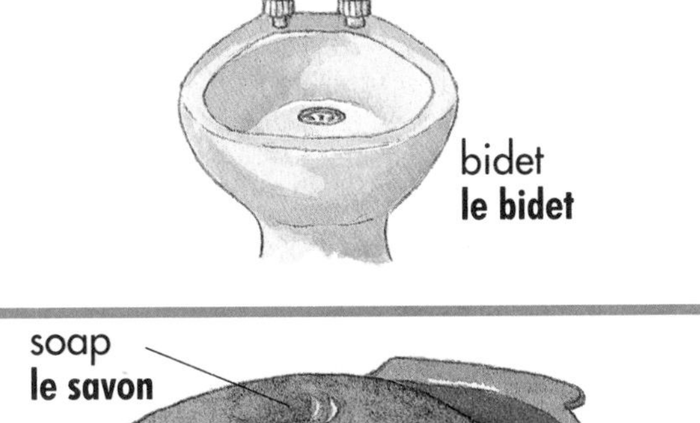

bidet
le bidet

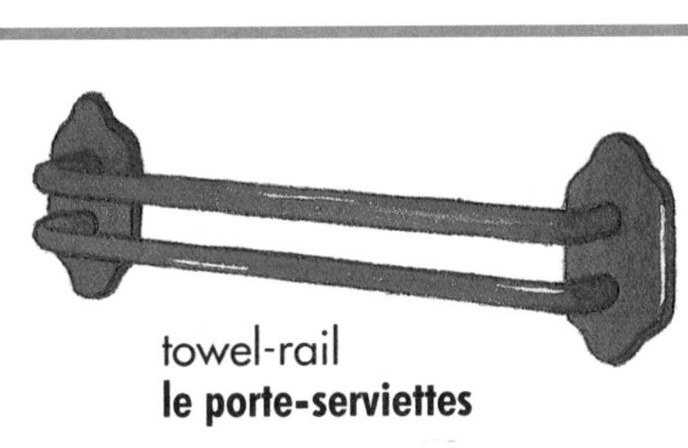

towel-rail
le porte-serviettes

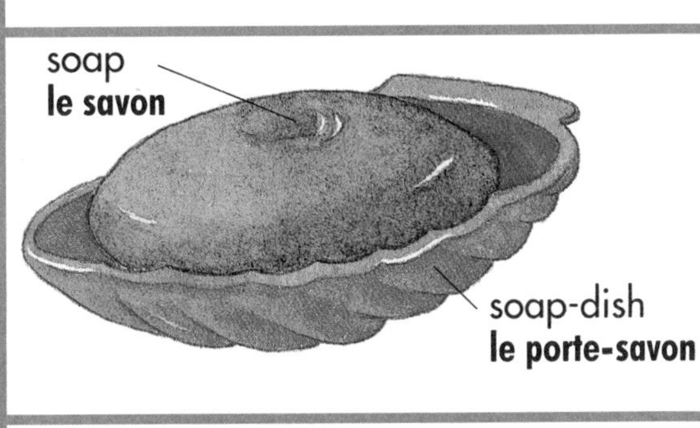

soap
le savon

soap-dish
le porte-savon

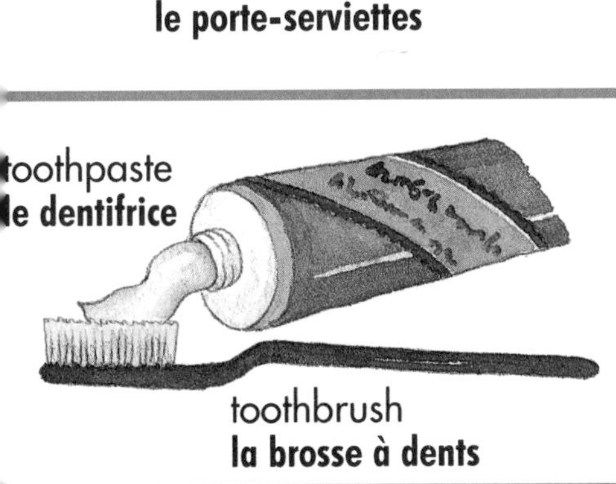

toothpaste
le dentifrice

toothbrush
la brosse à dents

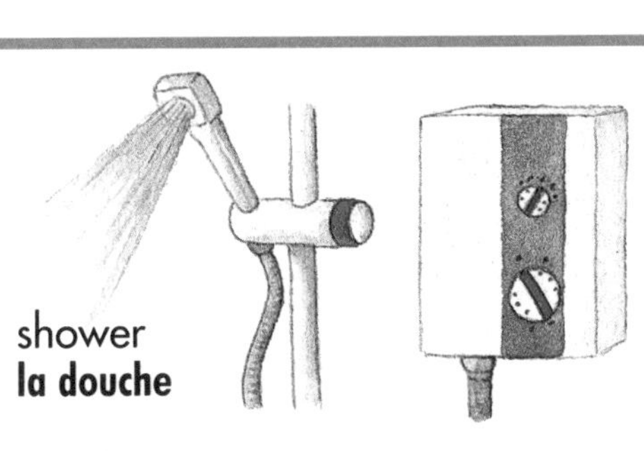

shower
la douche

tap
le robinet

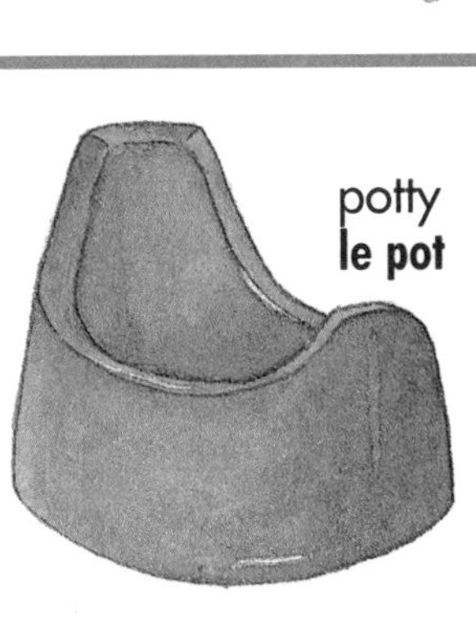

potty
le pot

the kitchen

food-mixer
le mixeur

kettle
la bouilloire

coffee pot
la cafetière

cupboard
le placard

cooker
la cuisinière

oven
le four

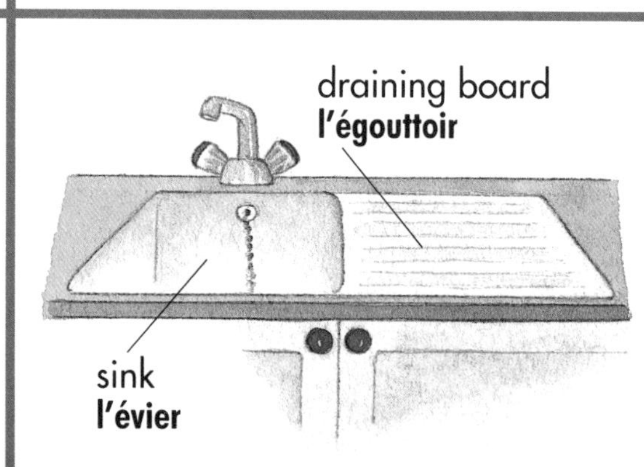

draining board
l'égouttoir

sink
l'évier

la cuisine

teapot
la théière

vacuum cleaner
l'aspirateur

iron
le fer à repasser

ironing board
la planche à repasser

washing machine
la machine à laver

dish-washer
le lave-vaisselle

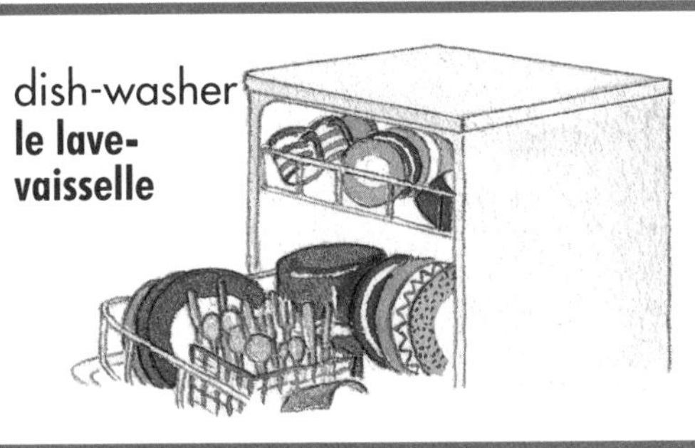

switch
l'interrupteur

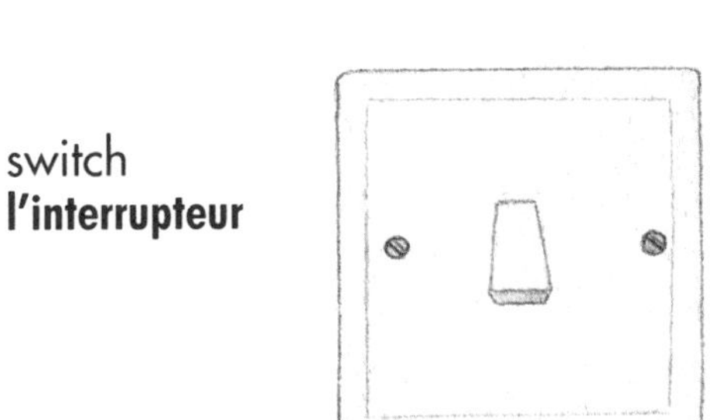

socket
la prise de courant

refrigerator/fridge
le réfrigérateur

freezer
le congélateur

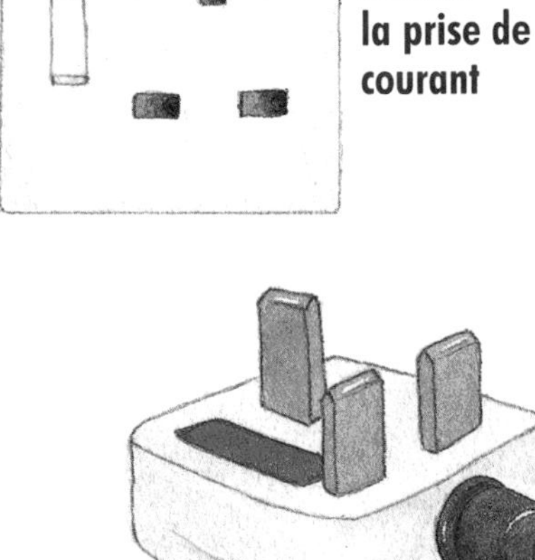

electric plug
la prise de courant

the living-room

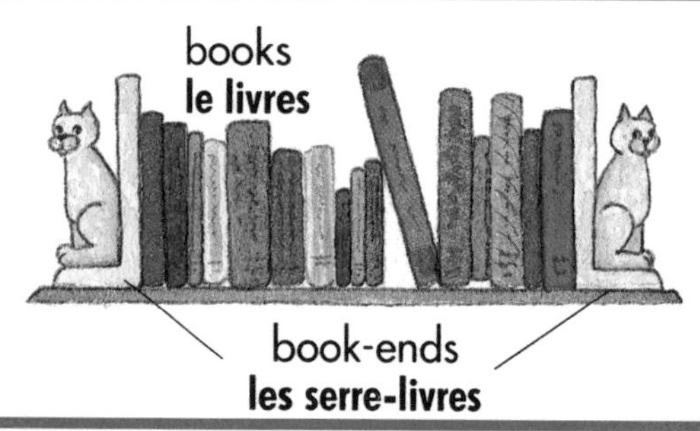

books
le livres

book-ends
les serre-livres

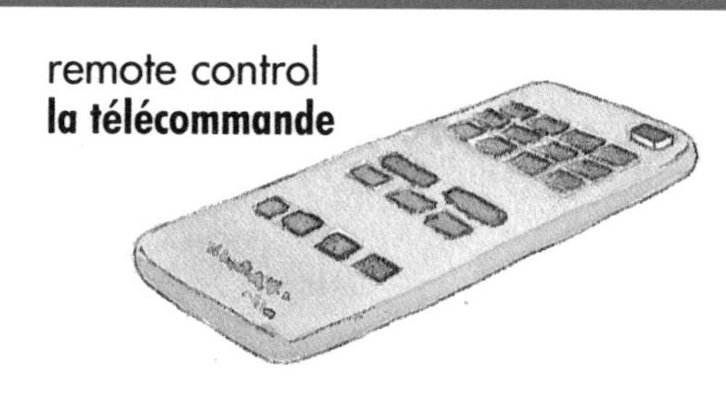

remote control
la télécommande

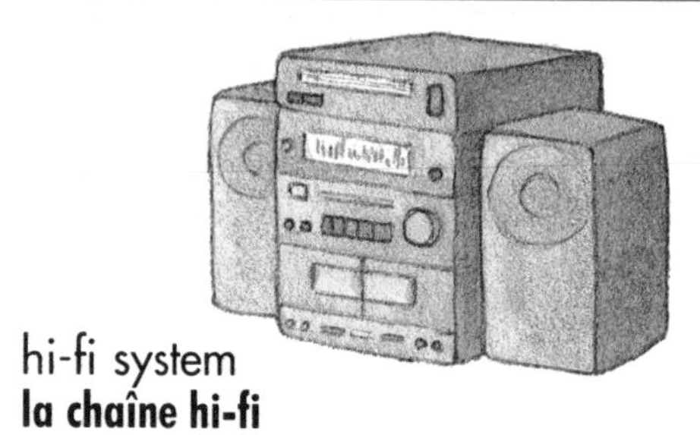

hi-fi system
la chaîne hi-fi

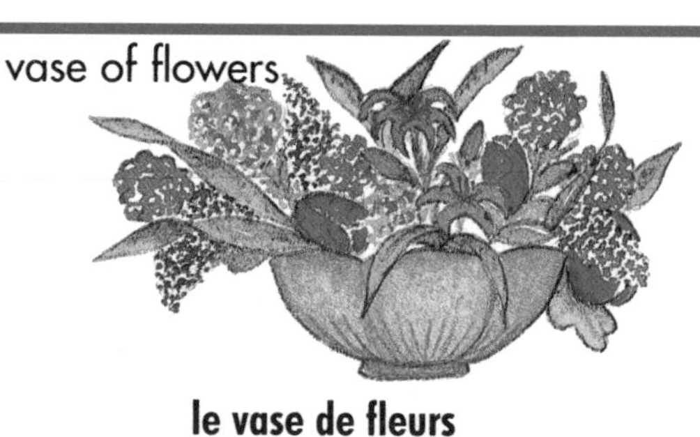

vase of flowers
le vase de fleurs

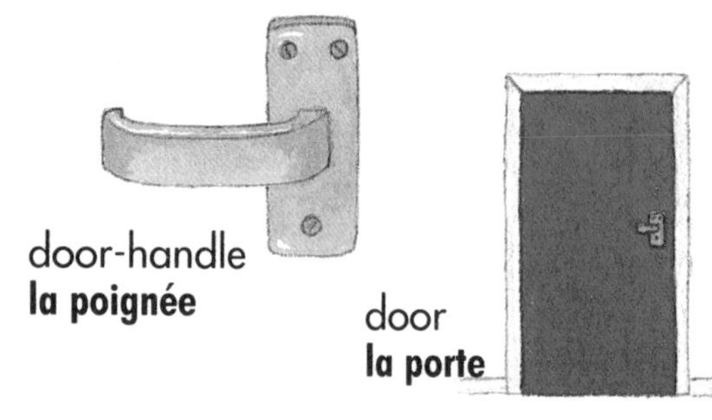

door-handle
la poignée

door
la porte

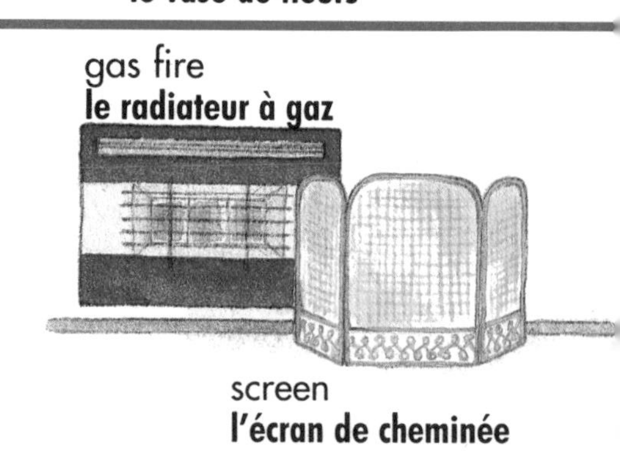

gas fire
le radiateur à gaz

screen
l'écran de cheminée

le salon

painting
le tableau

telephone/phone
le téléphone

magazine rack
le porte-magazines

newspapers
les journaux

comics
les bandes dessinées

magazines
les magazines

video cassette
la cassette vidéo

video recorder
le magnétoscope

television set/TV
le téléviseur/ la télévision

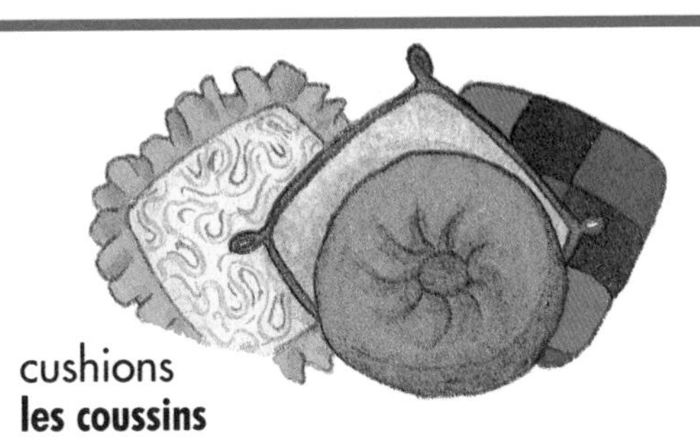

cushions
les coussins

photographs
les photos

mantlepiece
le dessus de cheminée

fireplace
la cheminée

radio
la radio

the dining-room

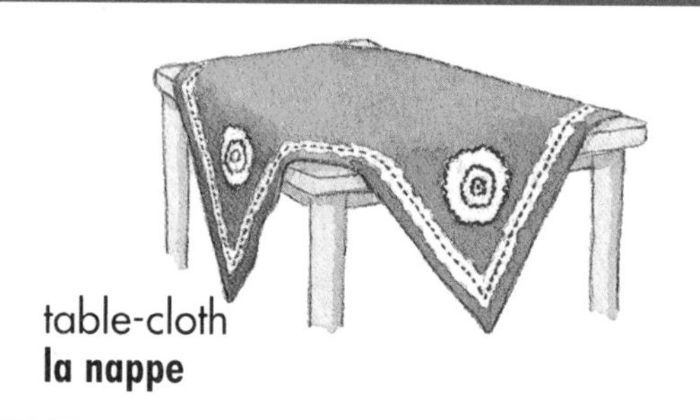

table-cloth
la nappe

plates
les assiettes

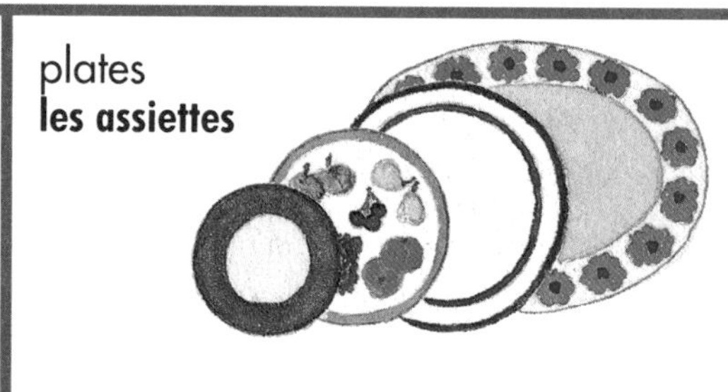

cup
la tasse

saucer
la soucoupe

teaspoon
la petite cuillère

oil
l'huile

vinegar
le vinaigre

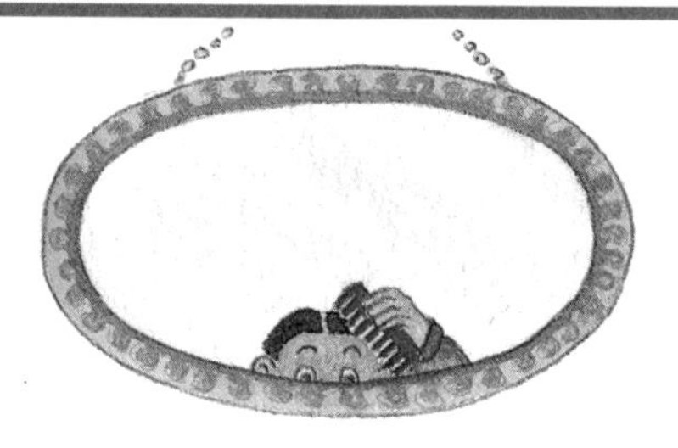

mirror
le miroir

la salle à manger

napkins
les serviettes

napkin ring
le rond de serviette

fork
la fourchette

table-mat
le set de table

spoon
la cuillère

knife
le couteau

candles
les bougies

candlestick
le bougeoir

salt
le sel

pepper
le poivre

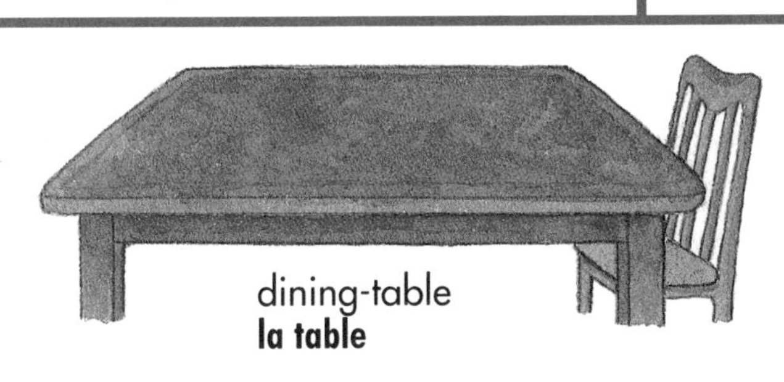

dining-table
la table

chairs
les chaises

eggcups
les coquetiers

jug
la carafe

tumbler
le verre

fruit bowl
la coupe de fruits

wine-glasses
les verres à vin

bottle
la bouteille

the playroom

toys
les jouets

rocking horse
le cheval à bascule

soft toys
les peluches

playpen
le parc pour enfants

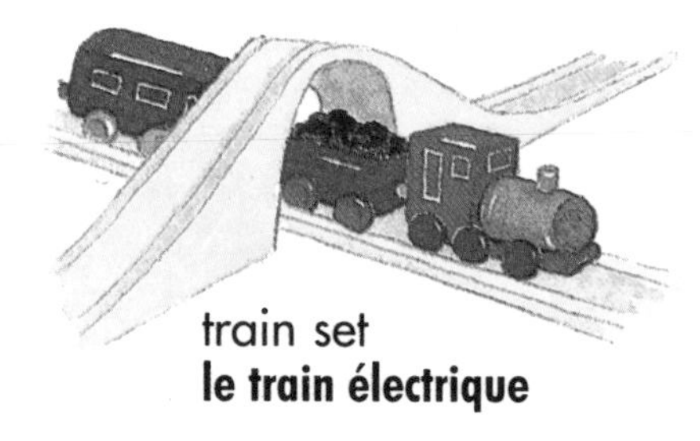

train set
le train électrique

building blocks
les cubes

toy soldiers
les petits soldats

fort
le fort

la salle de jeux

toy duck
le canard

toy boats
les bâteaux

spinning top
la toupie

teddy bear
l'ours en peluche

toy cars
les voitures

counting frame
le boulier compteur

skittles
les quilles

doll's house
la maison de poupée

playhouse
la maison (pliante)

doll's pram
le landau de poupée

things in the house

des choses chez nous

bookcase
la bibliothèque

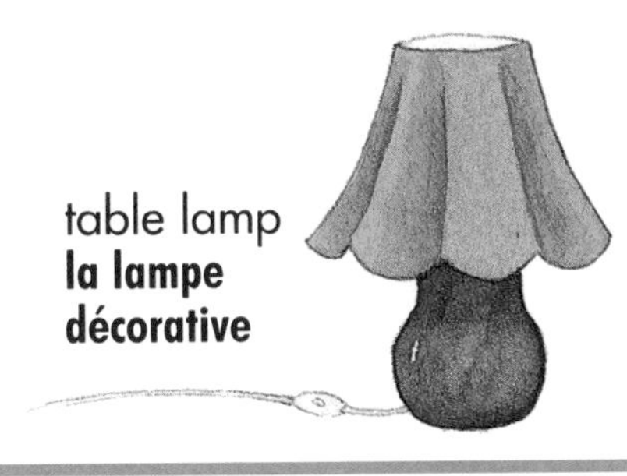

table lamp
la lampe décorative

sideboard
le buffet

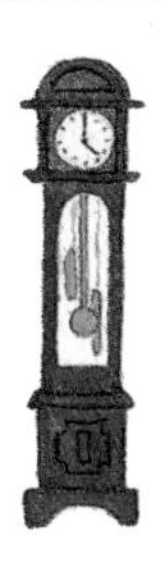

grandfather clock
l'horloge

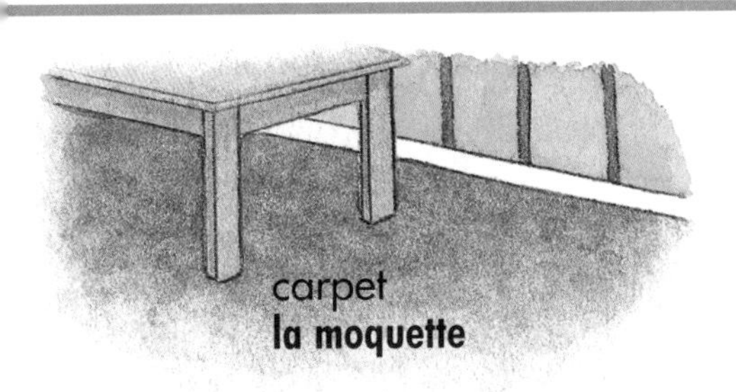

carpet
la moquette

coffee table
la table basse

candelabra
le candélabre

dressing-table
la coiffeuse

breakfast bar
la table du petit déjeuner

the garden

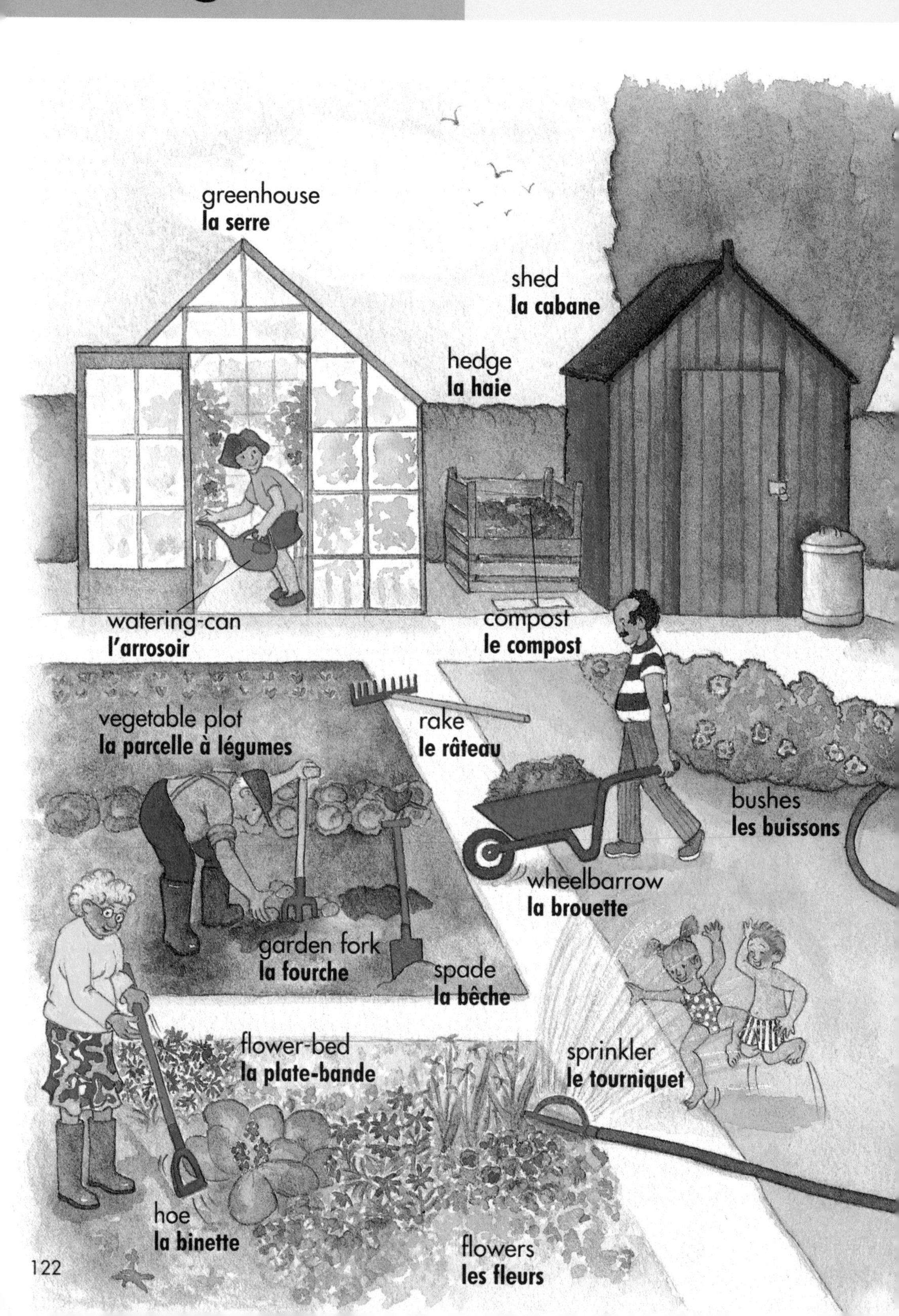
greenhouse
la serre
shed
la cabane
hedge
la haie
watering-can
l'arrosoir
compost
le compost
vegetable plot
la parcelle à légumes
rake
le râteau
bushes
les buissons
wheelbarrow
la brouette
garden fork
la fourche
spade
la bêche
flower-bed
la plate-bande
sprinkler
le tourniquet
hoe
la binette
flowers
les fleurs

chimney
la cheminée
TV aerial
l'antenne de télévision
bonfire
le feu
roof
le toit
drain-pipe
le tuyau
d'écoulement
gutter
la gouttière
porch
le porche
ladder
l'échelle
front
door
la porte
d'entrée
window box
la jardinière à
fleurs
barrel
le tonneau
roof tiles
les tuiles
grass lawn
la pelouse
path
l'allée
lawnmower
la tondeuse
hosepipe
le tuyau d'arrosage

in the workshop

paint-brushes
les pinceaux

saw
la scie

sandpaper
le papier de verre

paint pots
les pots de peinture

nuts and bolts

les boulons et les écrous

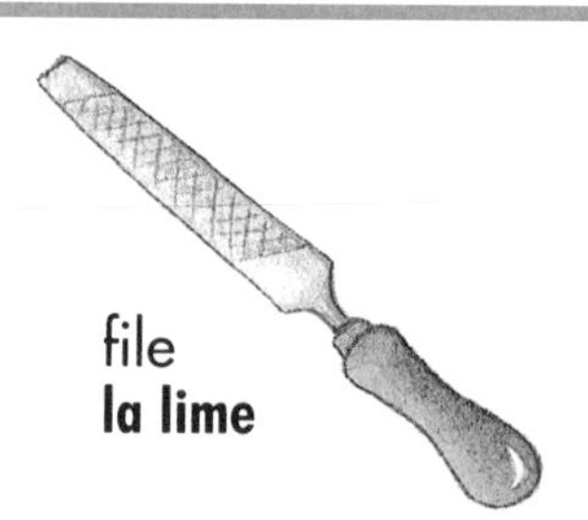

file
la lime

spanners
les clés

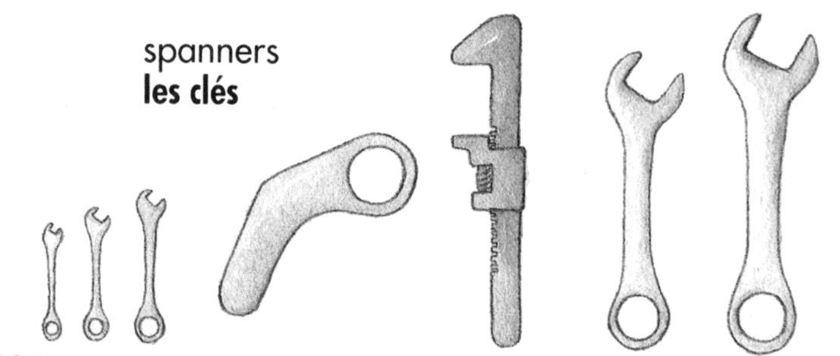

pickaxe
la pioche

oilcan
la burette d'huile

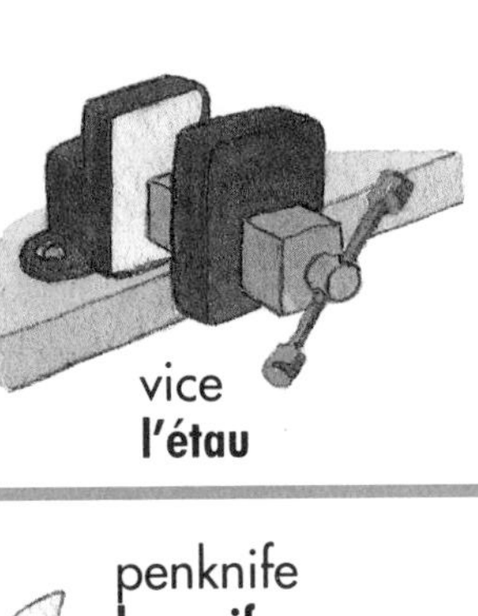
vice
l'étau

axe
la hache

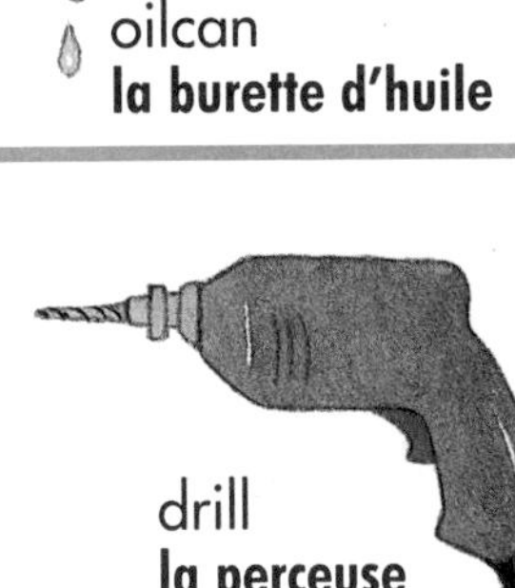
drill
la perceuse

penknife
le canif
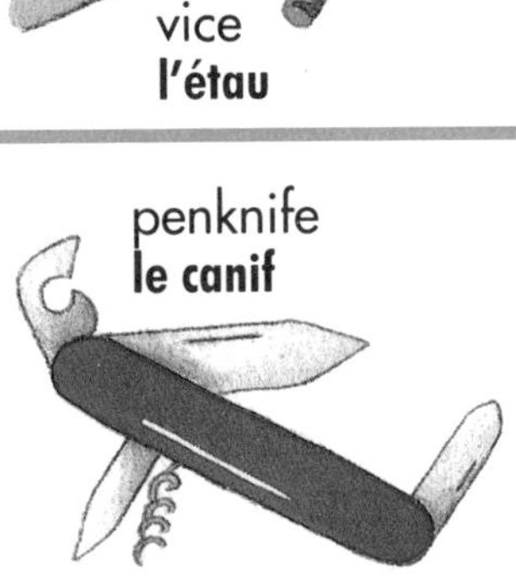

wooden plank
la planche

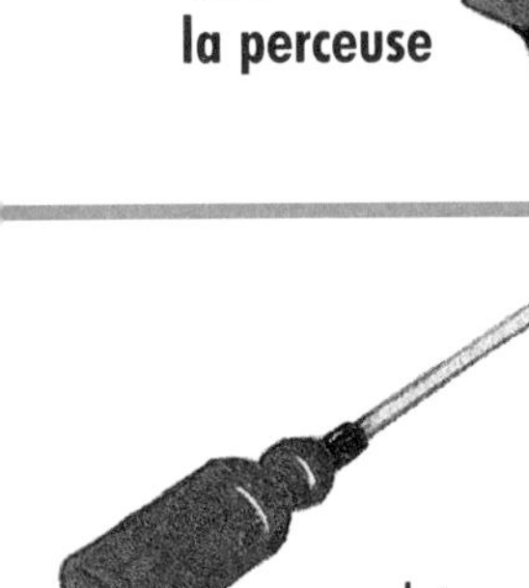
screwdriver
le tournevis

screws
les vis
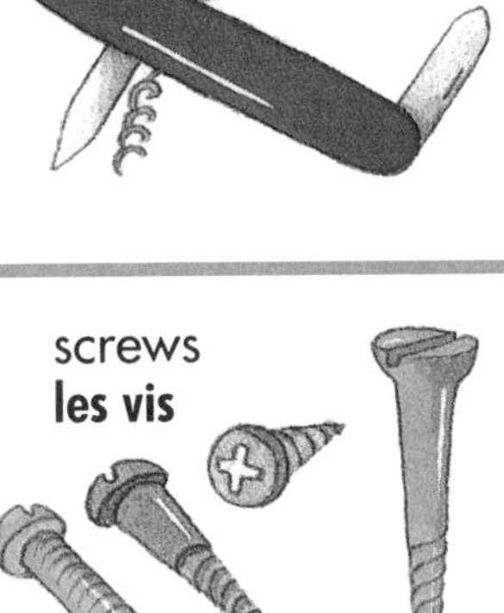

bucket
le seau

toolbox
la boîte à outils

plane
le rabot
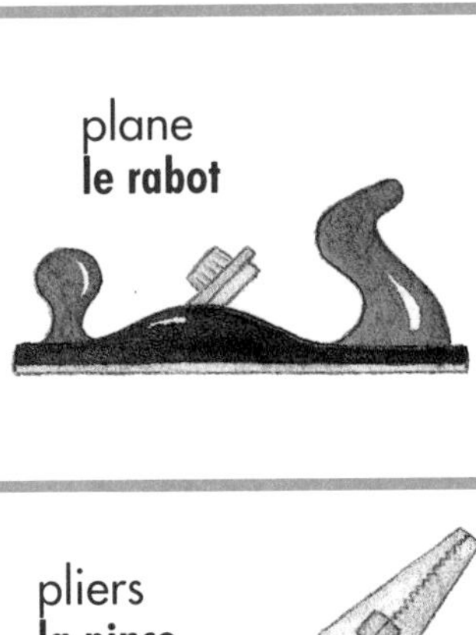

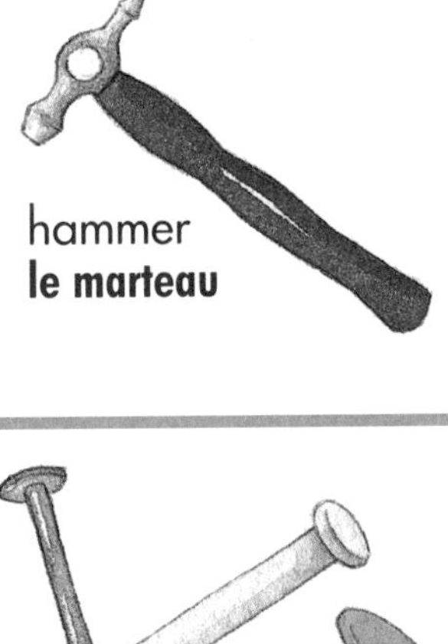
hammer
le marteau

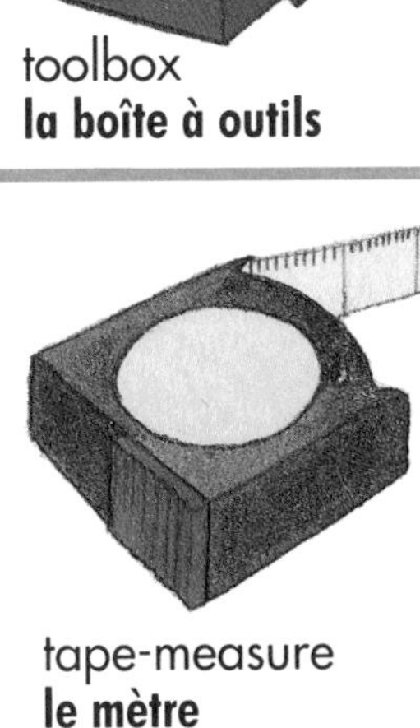
tape-measure
le mètre

pliers
la pince

nails
les clous

friendly pets

silkworm
le ver à soie
stick-insect
le phasme
pigeon
le pigeon
budgerigar
la perruche
canary
le canari
lizard
le lézard
lovebirds
les tourtereaux
mynah bird
le mynah
horse
le cheval
birdcage
la cage
parrot
le perroquet
Shetland pony
le poney de Shetland
foal
le poulain

the street

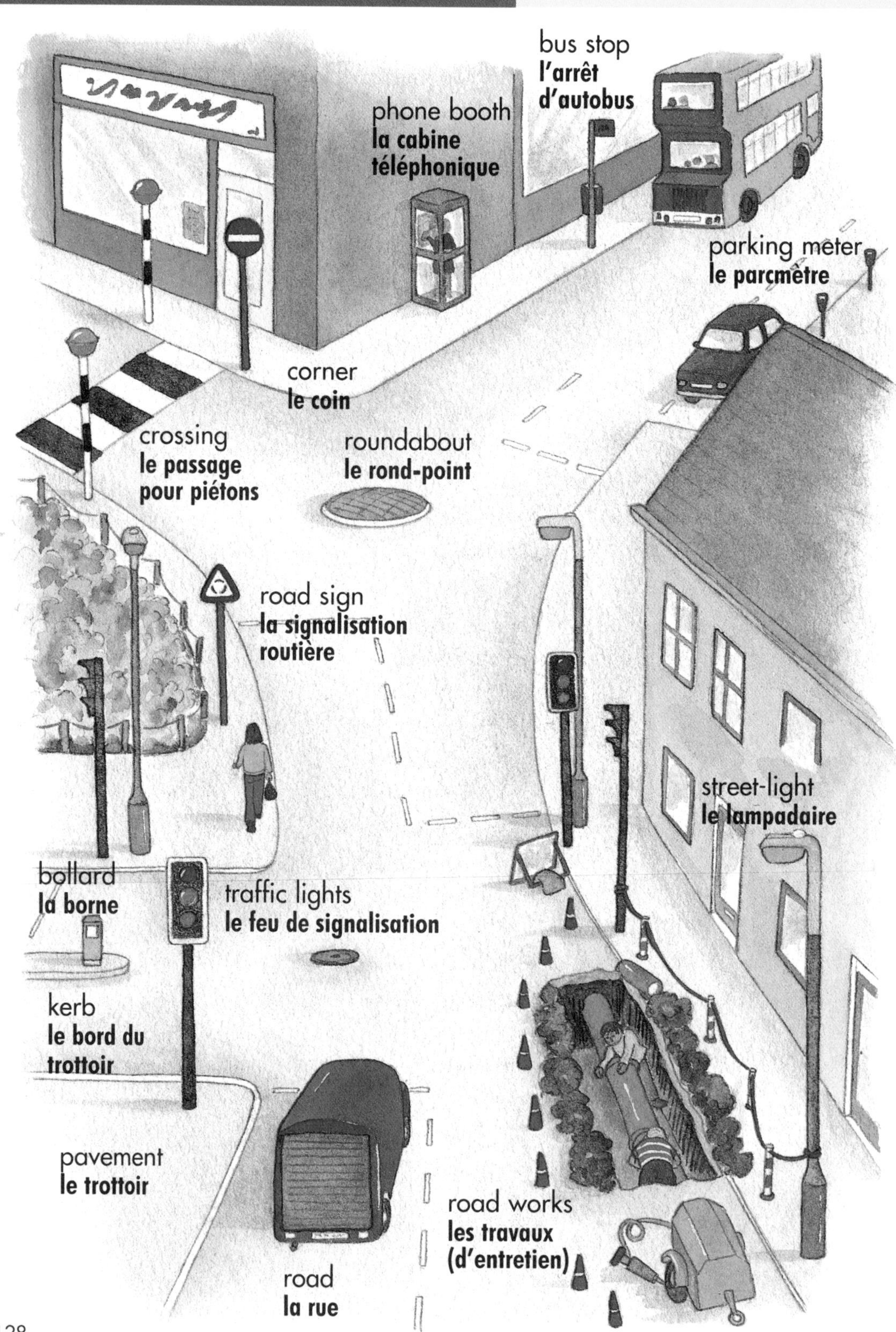

bus stop
l'arrêt d'autobus
phone booth
la cabine téléphonique
parking meter
le parcmètre
corner
le coin
crossing
le passage pour piétons
roundabout
le rond-point
road sign
la signalisation routière
street-light
le lampadaire
bollard
la borne
traffic lights
le feu de signalisation
kerb
le bord du trottoir
pavement
le trottoir
road works
les travaux (d'entretien)
road
la rue

la rue

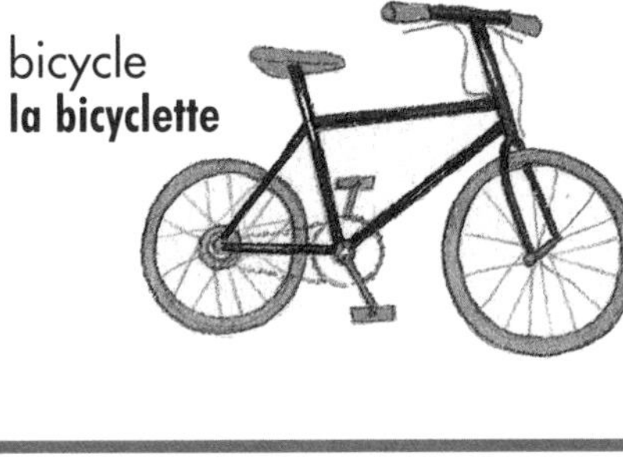

bicycle
la bicyclette

bus
le bus

fire-engine
le camion de pompiers

taxi
le taxi

car
la voiture

road-roller
le rouleau compresseur

lorry
le camion

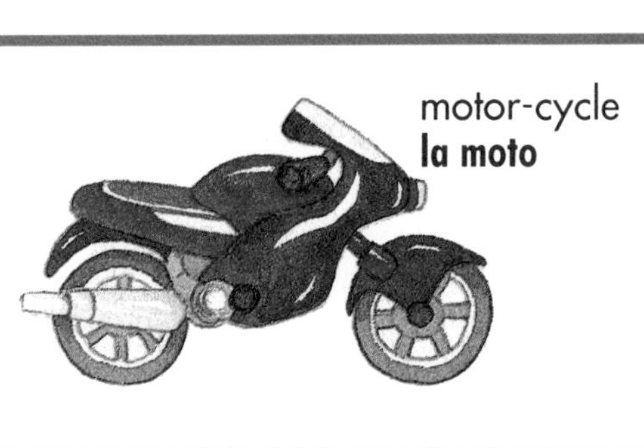

motor-cycle
la moto

olice car
a voiture de olice

van
la camionnette

in town

church
l'église

restaurant
le restaurant

market
le marché

houses
les maisons

hotel
l'hôtel

skyscraper
le gratte-ciel

post office
le bureau de poste

shop
le magasin

car park
le parking

theatre
le théâtre

en ville

bank
la banque

factory
l'usine

pub
le bar / le café

park
le jardin public

school
l'école

supermarket
le supermarché

library
la bibliothèque

cinema
le cinéma

police station
le poste de police

office block
l'immeuble de bureaux

in the supermarket

cheese
le fromage
butter
le beurre
milk
le lait
credit card
la carte de crédit
money
l'argent
receipt
le reçu
till
la caisse enregistreuse
check-out desk
la caisse
trolley
le caddie
handbag
le sac à main
purse
le porte-monnaie
shopping bag
le sac

some fruit — des fruits

orange
l'orange

grapes
le raisin

banana
la banane

cherries
les cerises

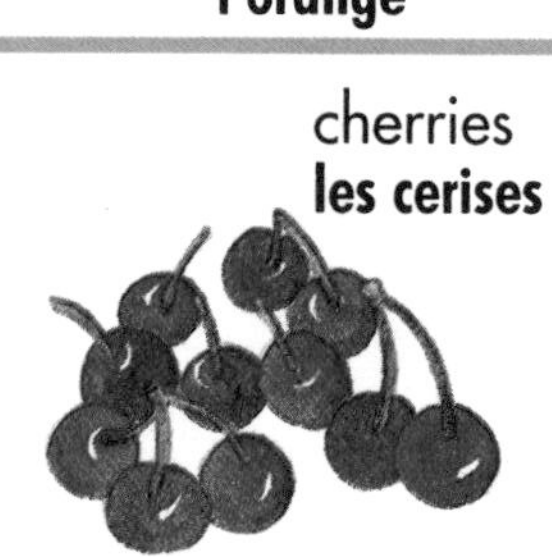

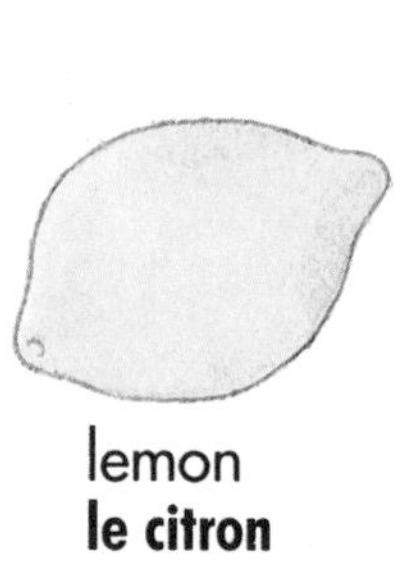

lemon
le citron

pineapple
l'ananas

apple
la pomme

redcurrants
les groseilles rouges

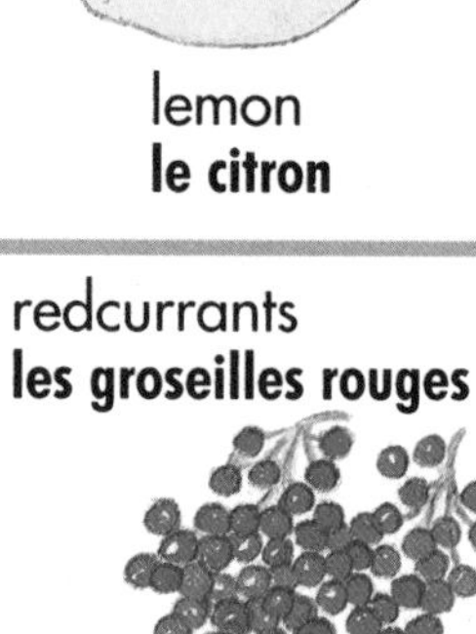

plums
les prunes

gooseberries
les groseilles à maquereau

grapefruit
le pamplemousse

pear
la poire

blackberries
les mûres

melon
le melon

strawberries
les fraises

des légumes — some vegetables

cabbage
le chou

tomatoes
les tomates

cucumber
le concombre

potatoes
les pommes de terre

pumpkin
la citrouille

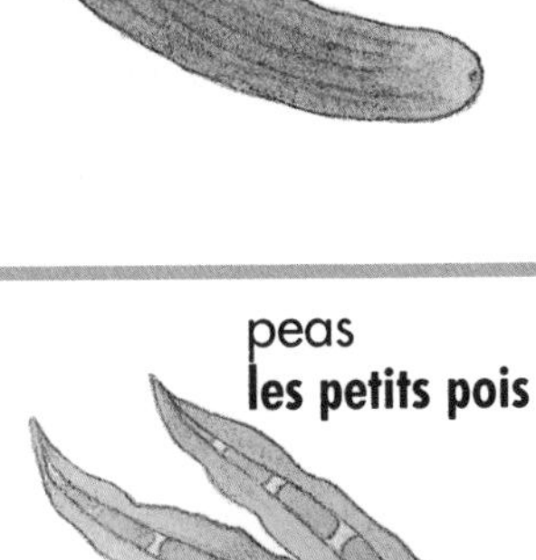

peas
les petits pois

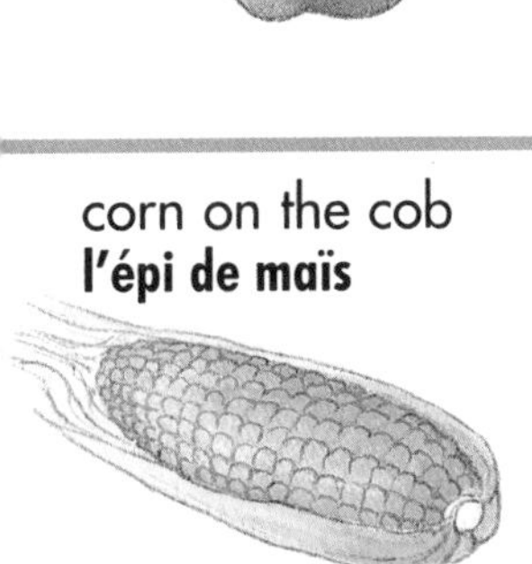

corn on the cob
l'épi de maïs

carrots
les carottes

onions
les oignons

leeks
les poireaux

green beans
les haricots verts

cauliflower
le chou-fleur

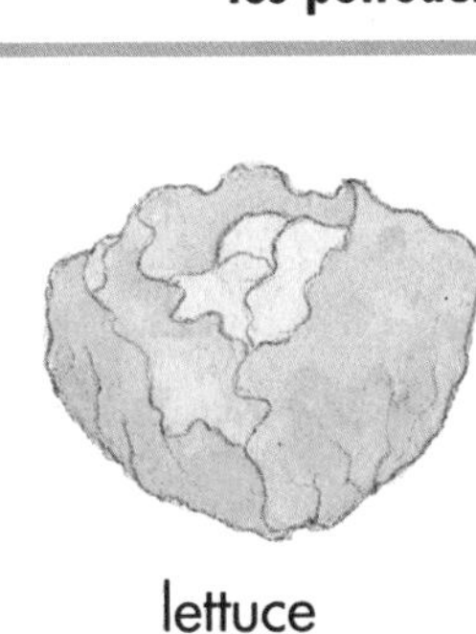

lettuce
la laitue

mushrooms
les champignons

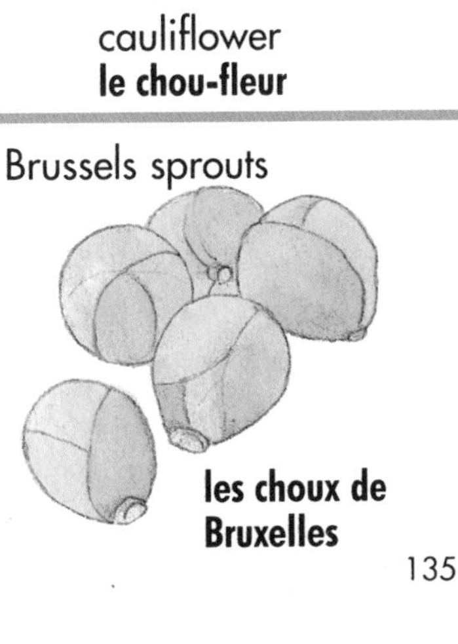

Brussels sprouts
les choux de Bruxelles

more things to eat and drink

d'autres choses à manger

fun in the park

au jardin public

people at work

actor
l'acteur

musician
la musicienne

secretary
la secrétaire

gardener
le jardinier

decorator
le peintre

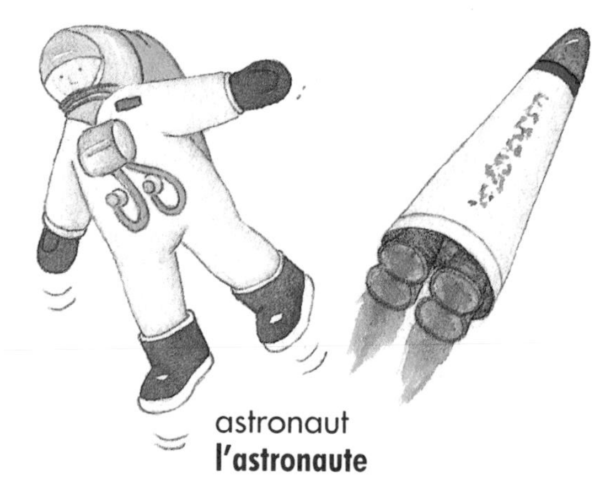

astronaut
l'astronaute

shop-keeper
le commerçant

diver
le plongeur

cook
le cuisinier

les gens au travail

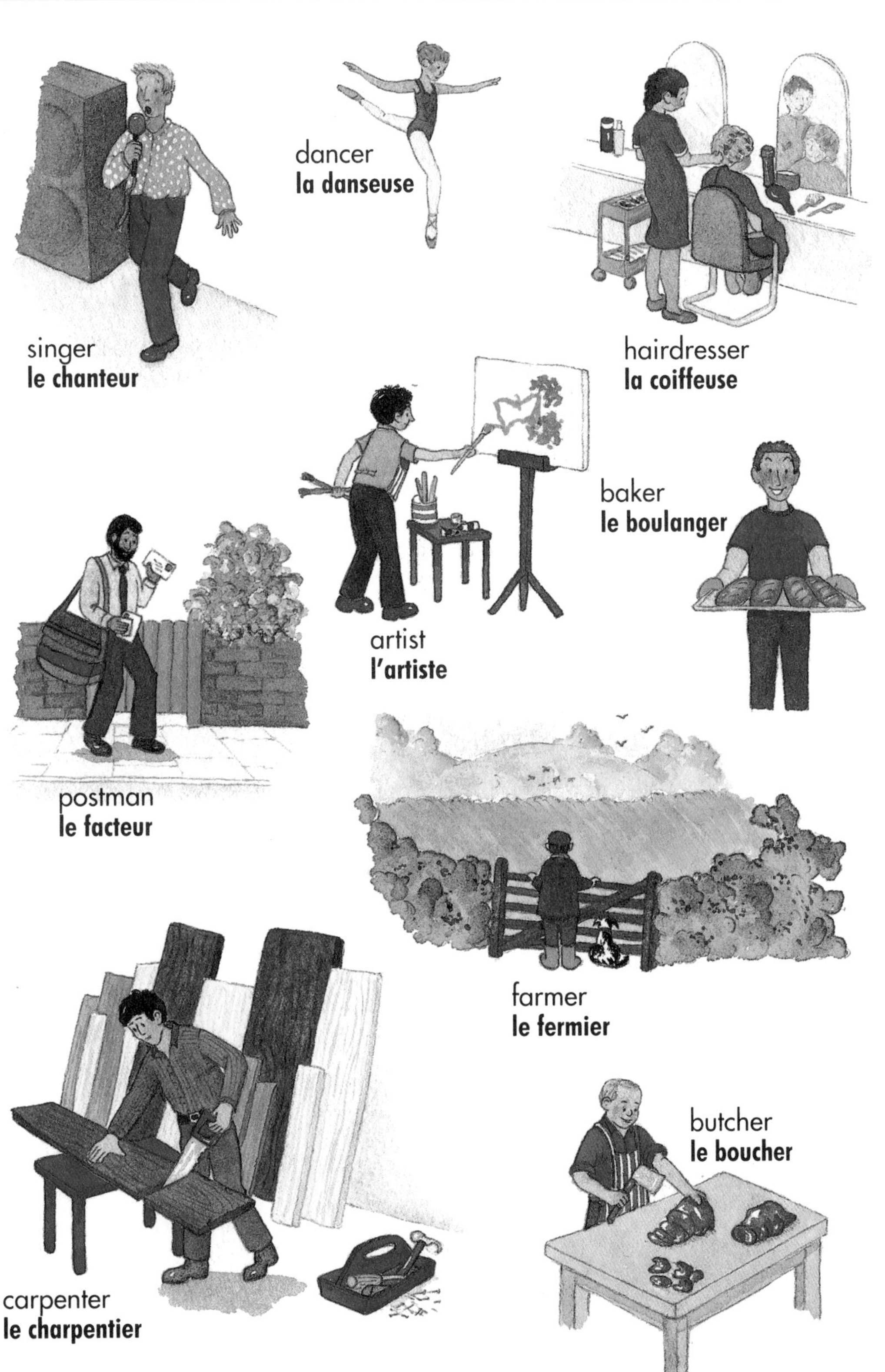

more people at work

clown
le clown

judge
le juge

porter
le porteur

TV announcer
la speakerine/
la présentatrice

window cleaner
le laveur de vitres

doctor
le docteur

fireman
le pompier

scientist
le scientifique

electrician
l'électricien

in the office

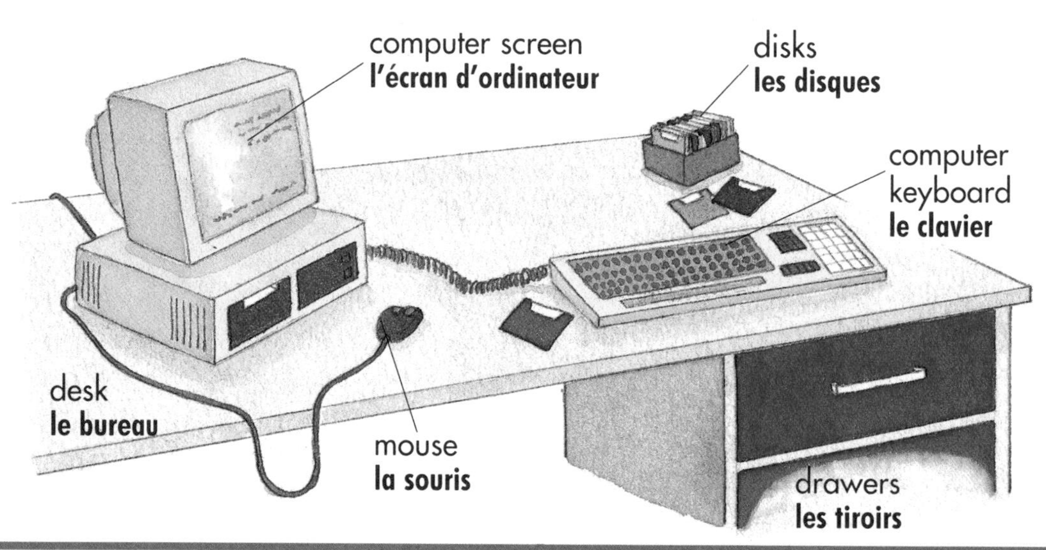

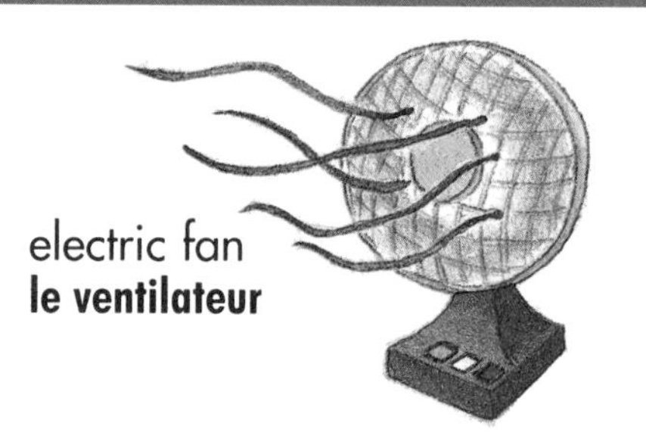

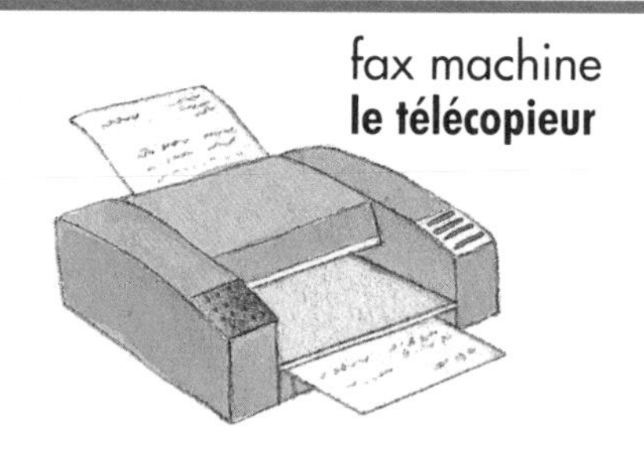

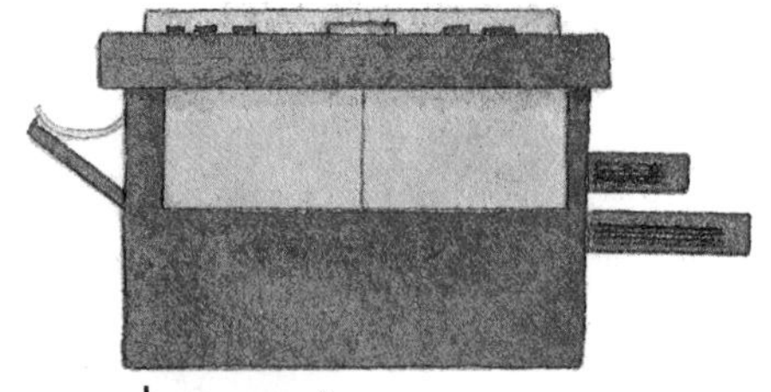

photocopier
la machine à photocopier

envelopes
les enveloppes

au bureau

calendar
le calendrier

filing cabinet
le classeur

pencil
le crayon

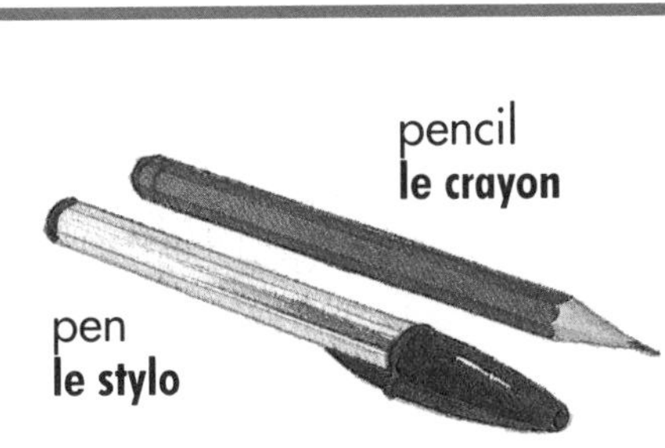

pen
le stylo

pencil sharpener
le taille-crayon

rubber
la gomme

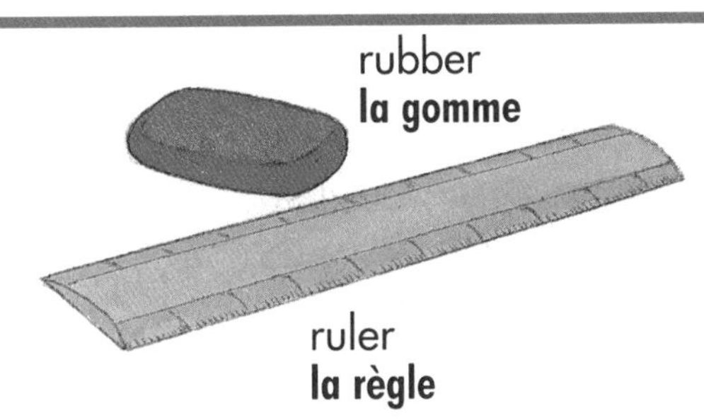

ruler
la règle

stapler
l'agrafeuse

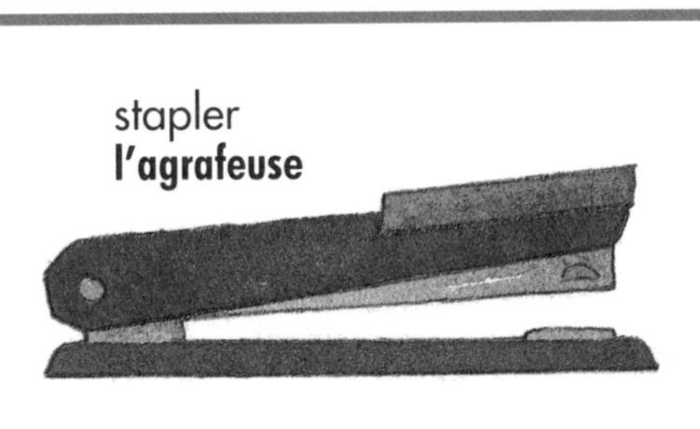

paperweight
le presse-papiers

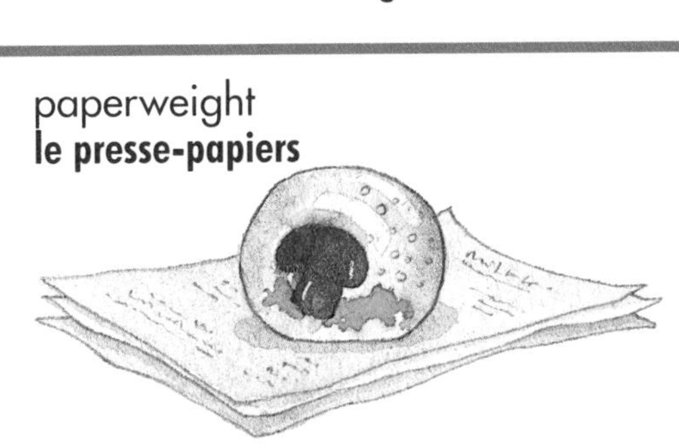

calculator
la calculette

wastepaper bin
la corbeille à papier

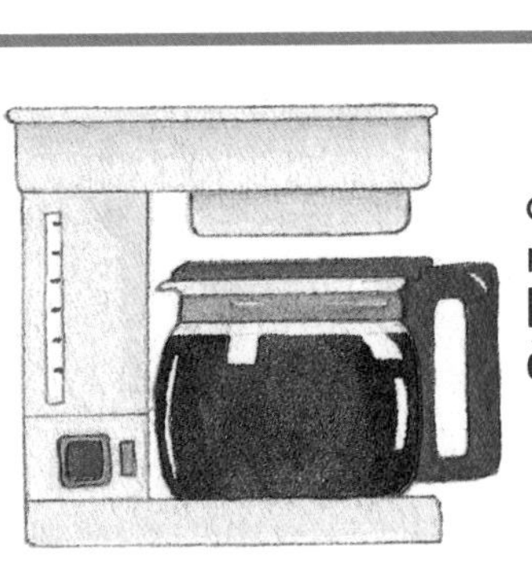

coffee
machine
**la machine
à café**

at the garage

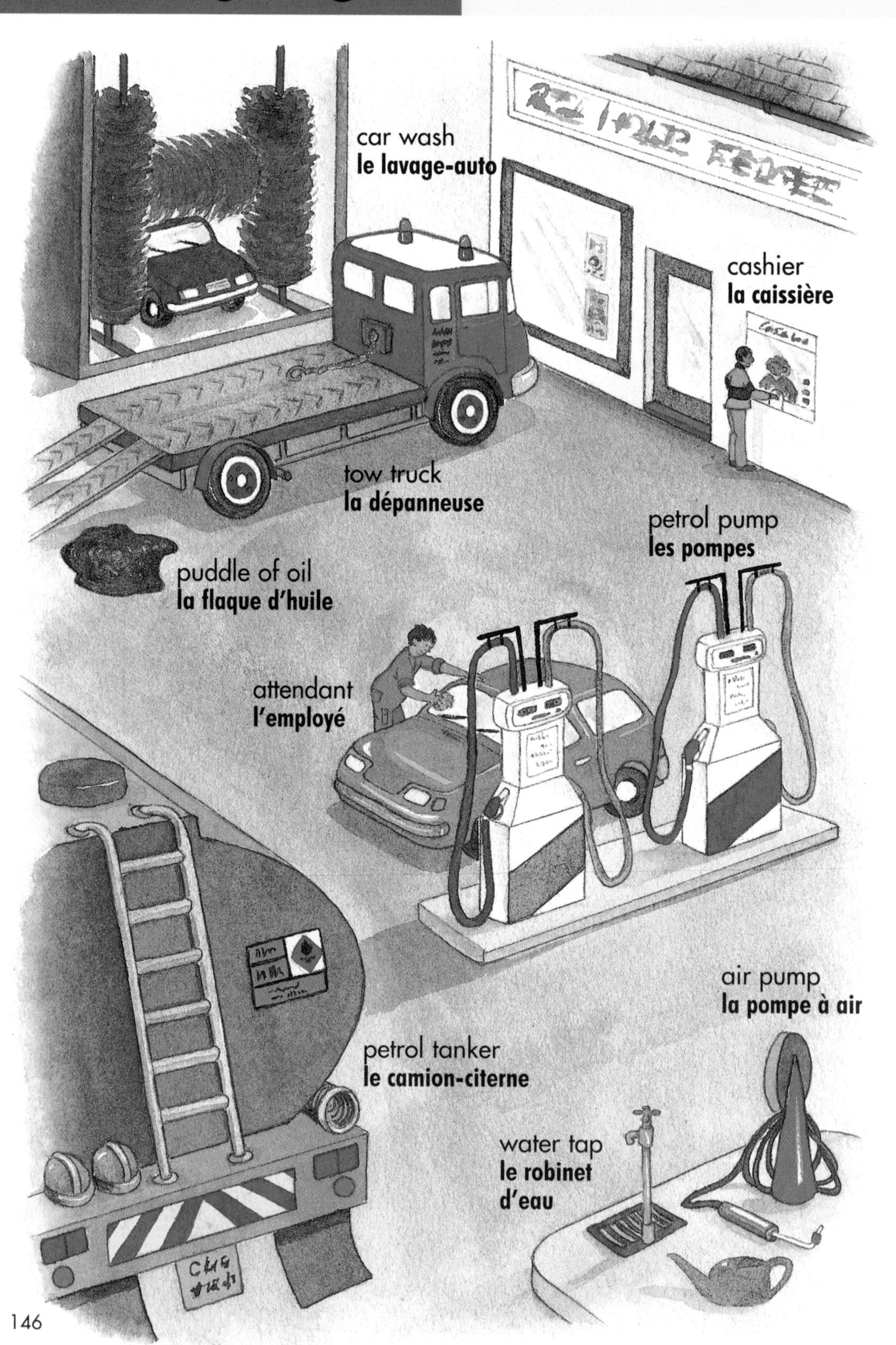

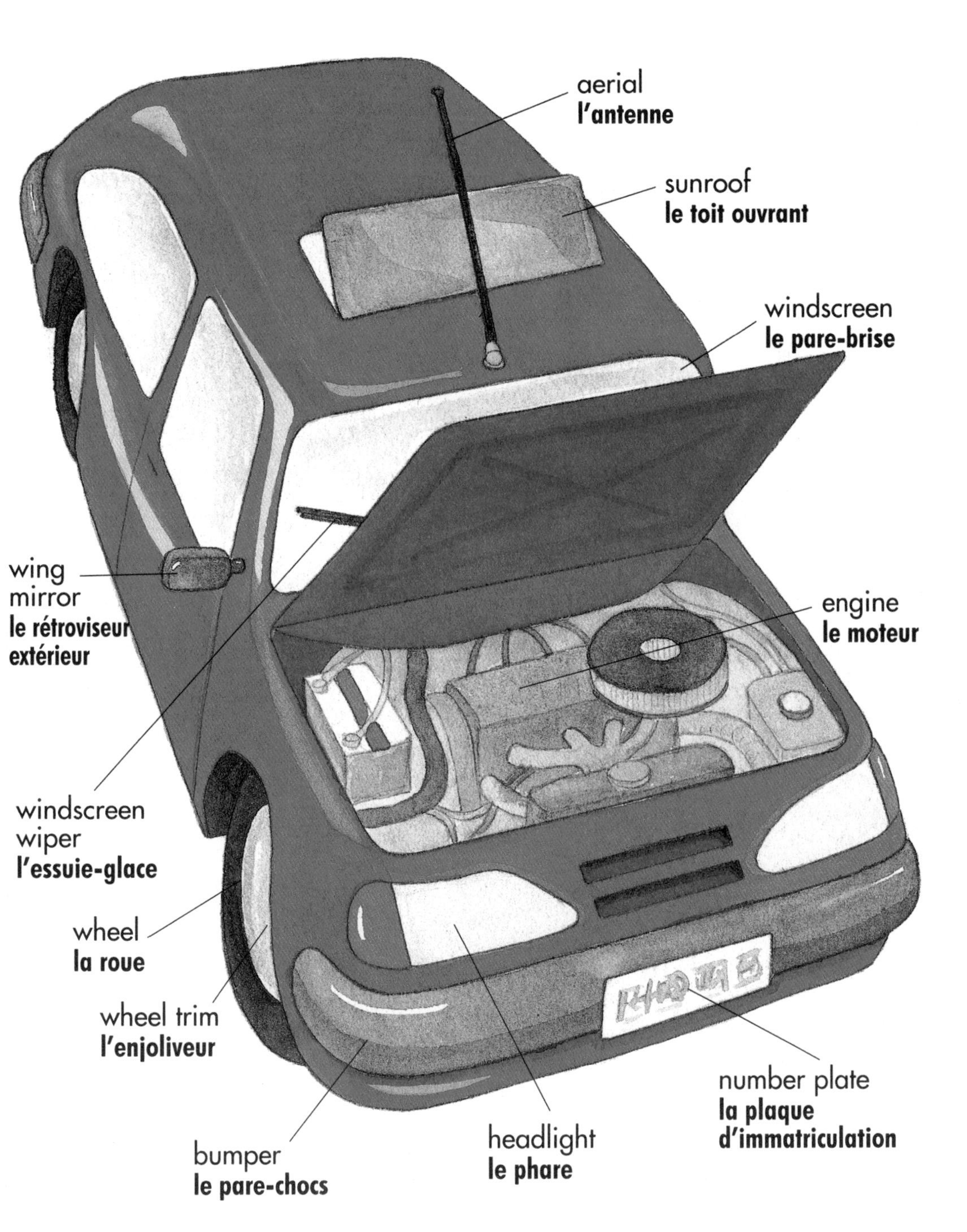
aerial
l'antenne
sunroof
le toit ouvrant
windscreen
le pare-brise
wing mirror
le rétroviseur extérieur
engine
le moteur
windscreen wiper
l'essuie-glace
wheel
la roue
wheel trim
l'enjoliveur
number plate
la plaque d'immatriculation
headlight
le phare
bumper
le pare-chocs

at the doctor chez le docteur

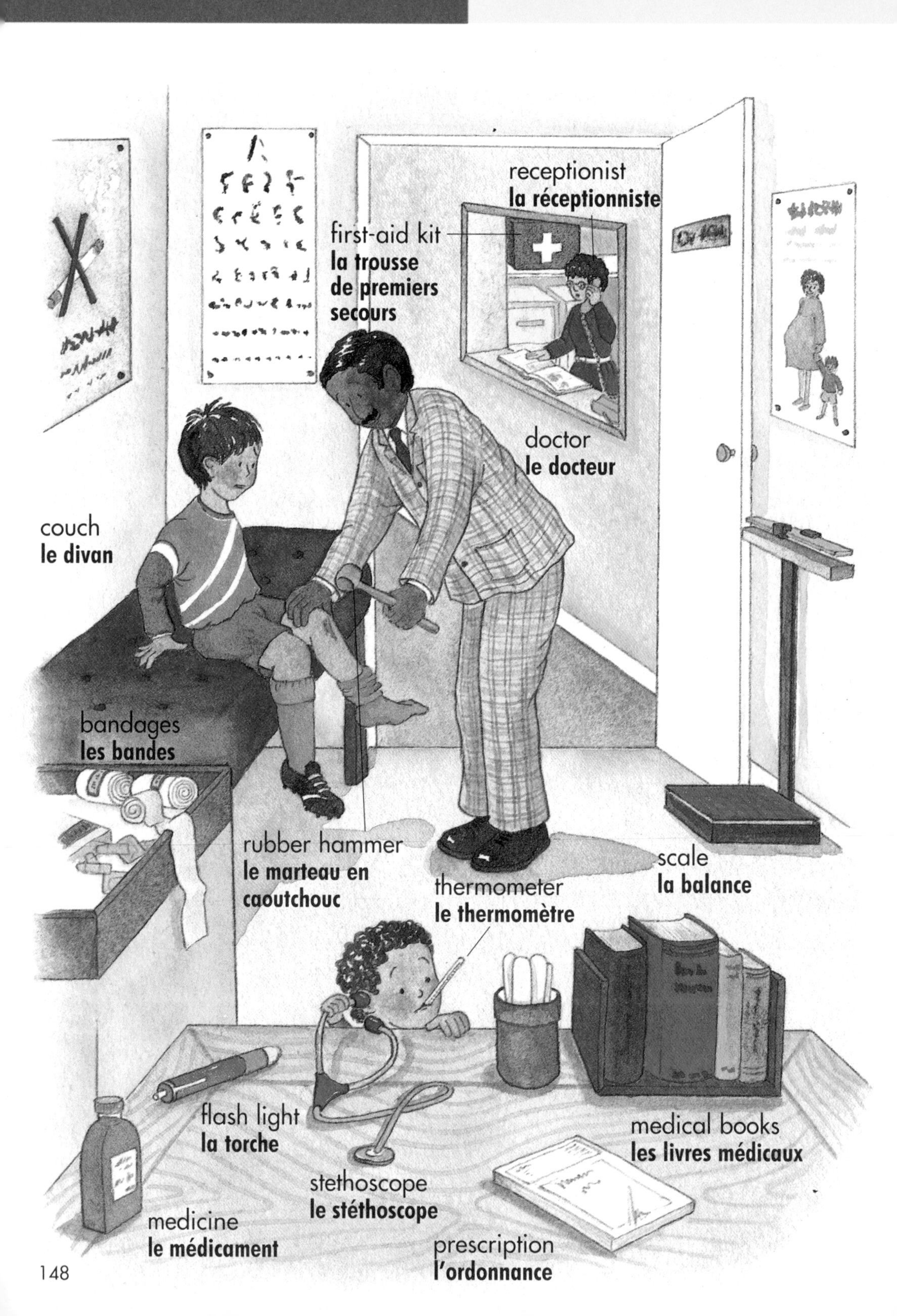

chez le dentiste

at the dentist

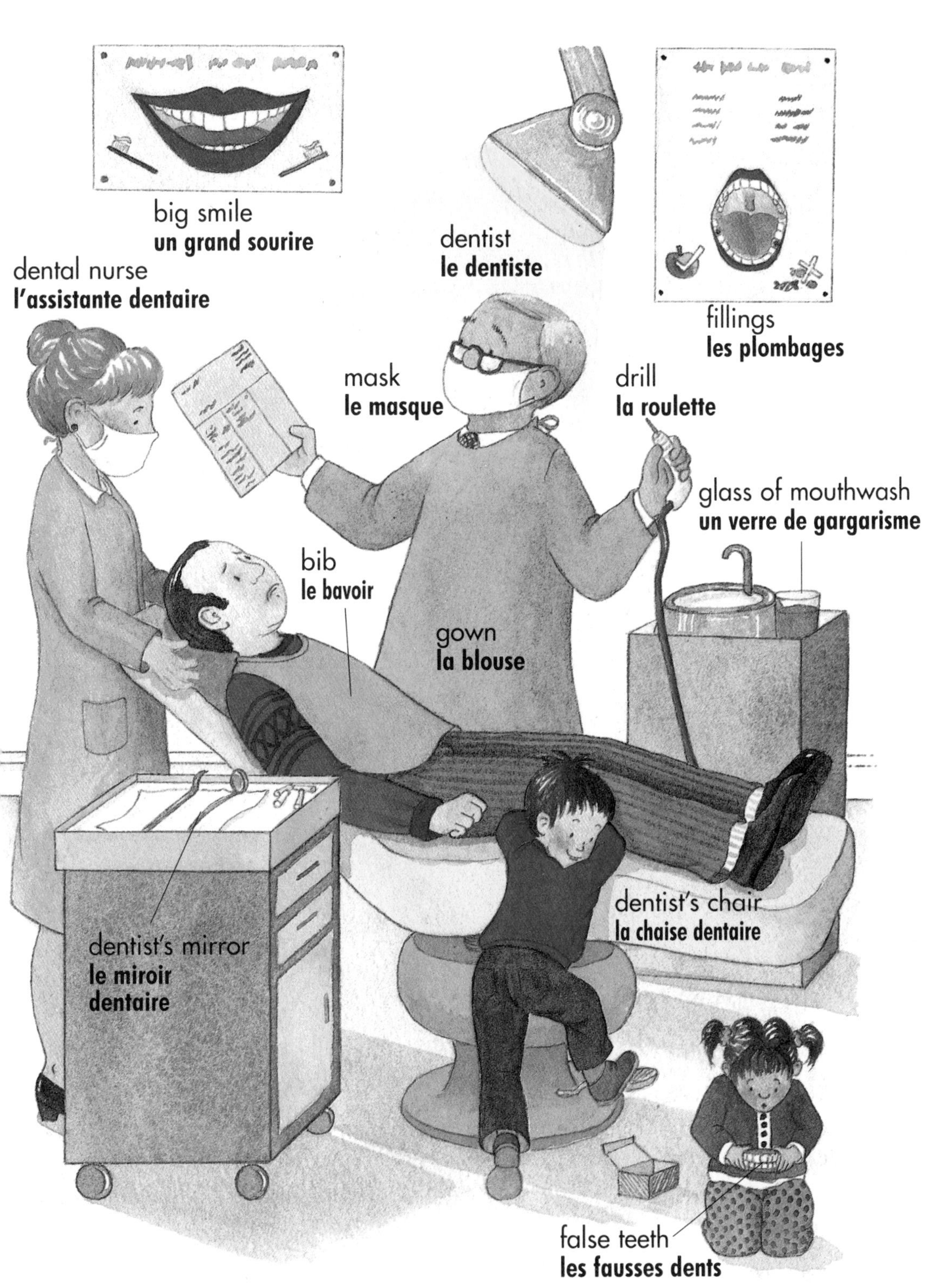

in hospital

doctor
le médecin
ambulance
l'ambulance
crutches
les béquilles
vase of flowers
un vase de fleurs
glass of orange juice
un verre de jus d'orange
locker
le casier
cast
le plâtre
hospital bed
le lit d'hôpital
orderly
l'aide-soignant
wheelchair
le fauteuil roulant
bedpan
le bassin hygiénique
trolley
le chariot

X-RAY DEPT.
DO NOT ENTER WHEN RED LIGHT IS ON
x-ray machine
la machine à radiographier
x-ray
la radio
curtain
le rideau
consultant
le médecin consultant
nurse
l'infirmière
syringe
la seringue
tray
le plateau
potty
le pot
slippers
les pantoufles
scissors
les ciseaux

games and pastimes

reading
lire

blindman's buff
colin-maillard

writing
écrire

dressing-up
se déguiser

singing
chanter

sewing
coudre

board game
un jeu de société

collecting stamps
la philatélie

sleeping
dormir

chess
les échecs

computer game
le jeu sur ordinateur

walking
marcher

listening to music
écouter de la musique

dancing
danser

playing cards
les cartes à jouer

leapfrog
le saute-mouton

gardening
le jardinage

making music
faire de la musique

canoeing
l'aviron
American football
le football américain
diving
le plongeon
tennis
le tennis
showjumping
le concours hippique
basketball
le basketball
skating
le patinage
rugby
le rugby
cycling
le cyclisme

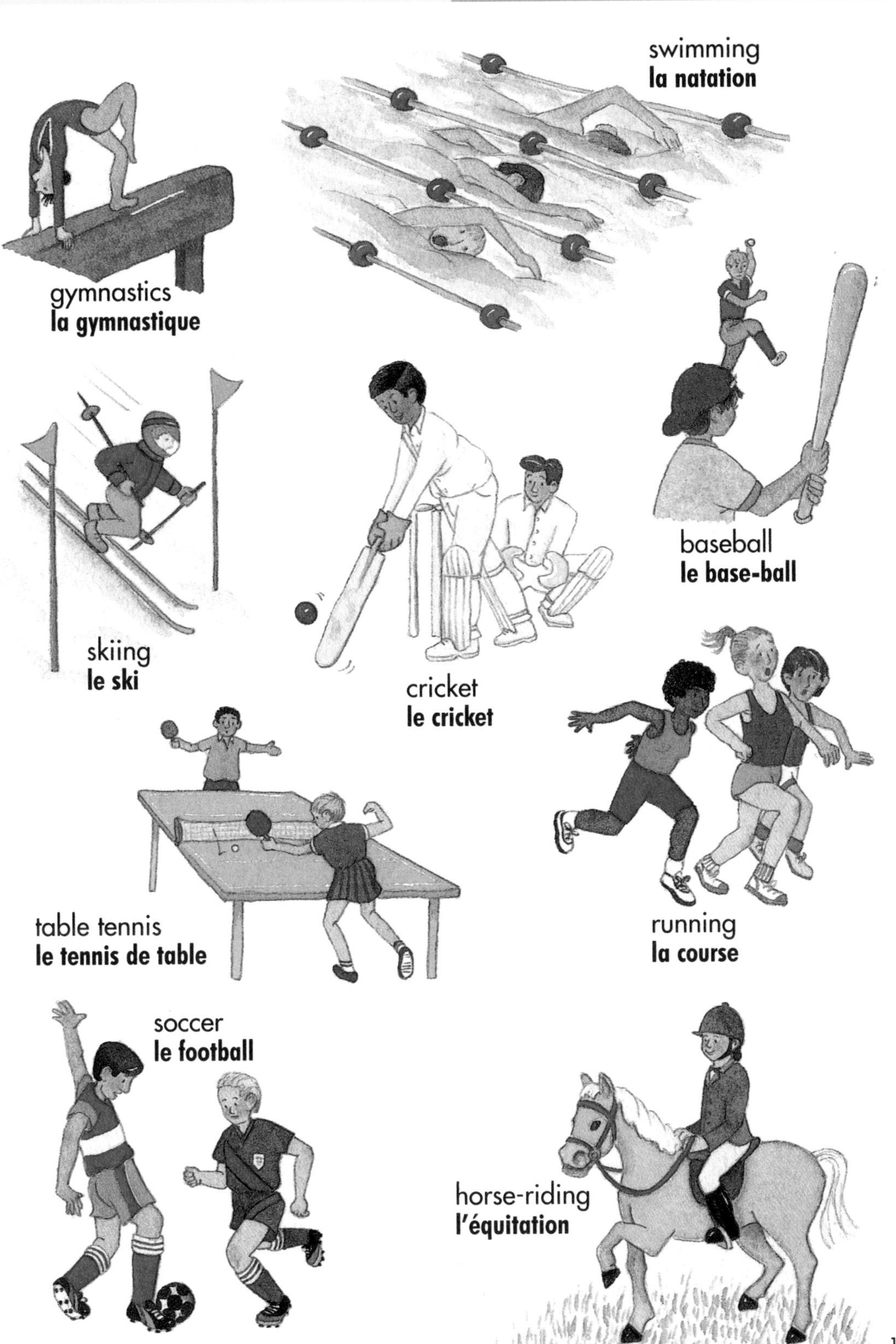
swimming
la natation
gymnastics
la gymnastique
baseball
le base-ball
skiing
le ski
cricket
le cricket
table tennis
le tennis de table
running
la course
soccer
le football
horse-riding
l'équitation

on the farm

sheep
le mouton

lamb
l'agneau

cow
la vache

calf
le veau

ducklings
les canetons

duck
le canard

milk
containers
**les bidons
de lait**

orchard
le verger

cockerel
le coq

à la ferme

haystack
la meule de foin

turkey
le dindon

goslings
les oisons

goose
l'oie

foal
le poulain

horse
le cheval

bull
le taureau

tractor
le tracteur

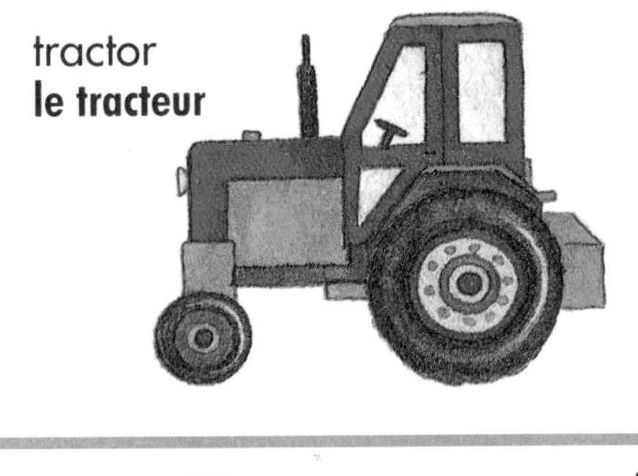

kid
le chevreau

goat
la chèvre

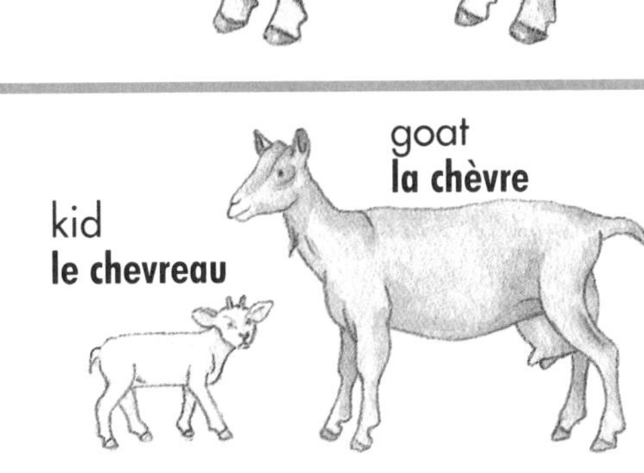

pig
le cochon

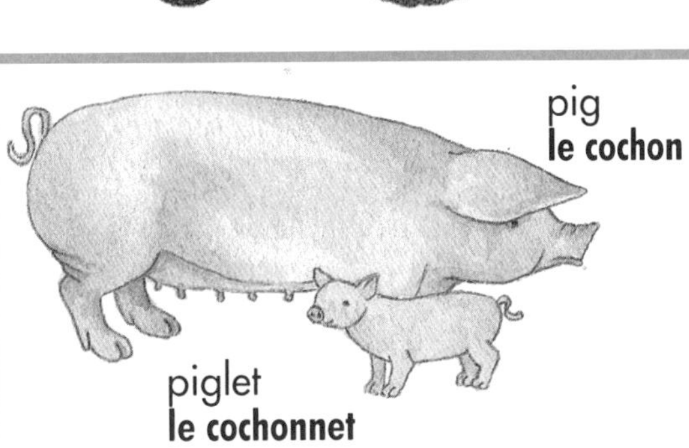

piglet
le cochonnet

hen
la poule

chicks
les poussins

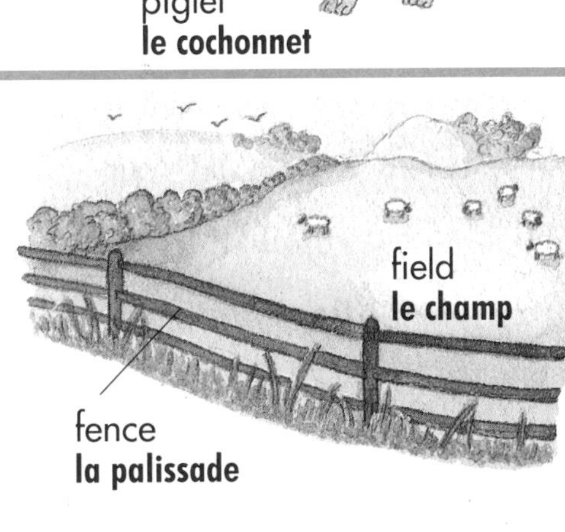

field
le champ

fence
la palissade

at school

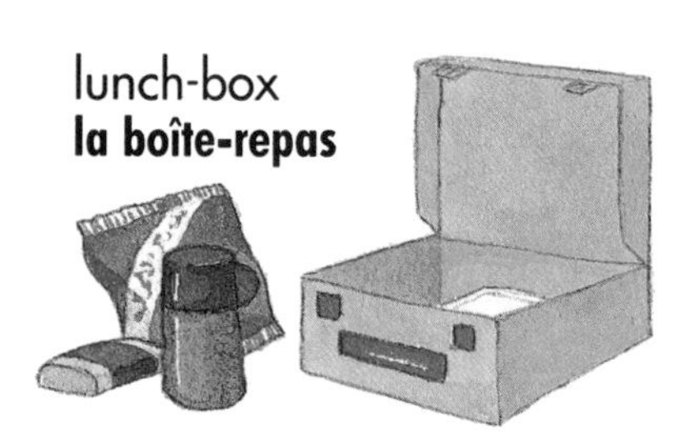

lunch-box
la boîte-repas

pupils
les élèves

globe
la mappemonde

pot of paste
le pot de colle

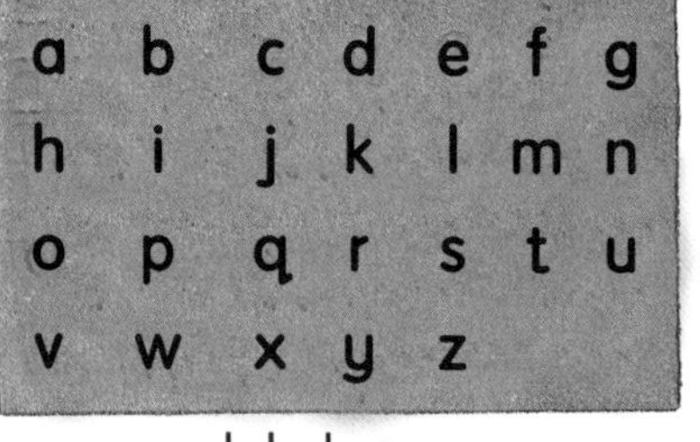

alphabet
l'alphabet

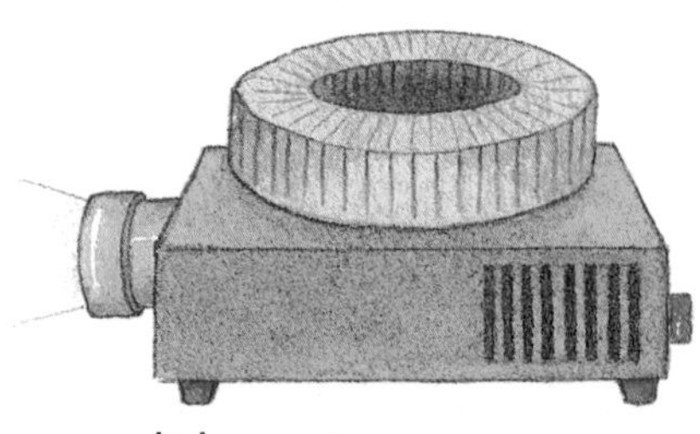

slide projector
le projecteur de diapositives

à l'école

wall chart
la planche murale

notebook
le cahier

satchel
le cartable

drawing
le dessin

modelling clay
la pâte à modeler

blackboard
le tableau noir

teacher
l'institutrice

easel
le chevalet

chalks
les craies

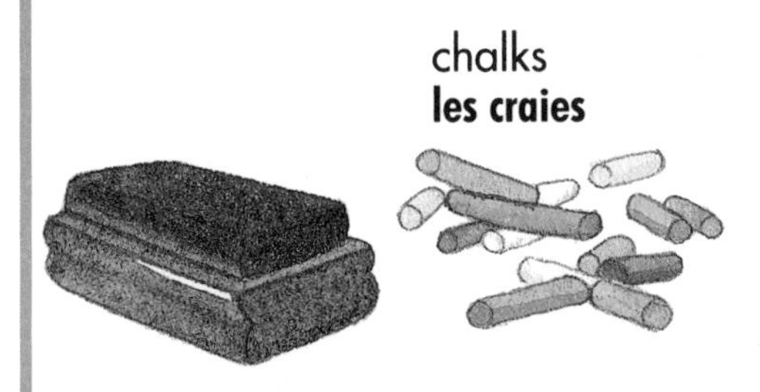

pencil case
la trousse

writing
l'écriture

going places: by train

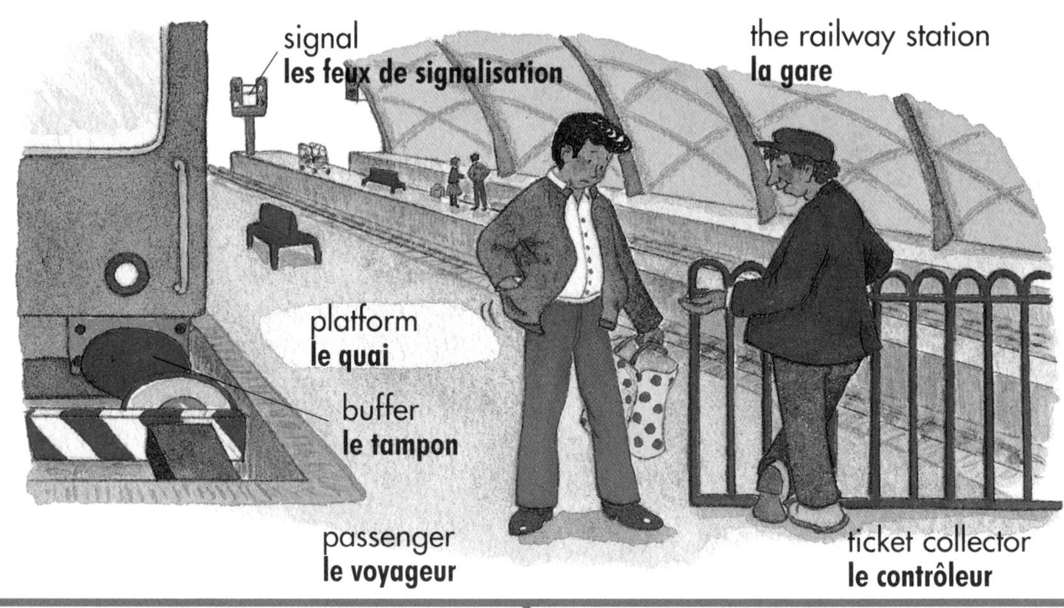

aller en train

ticket office
le guichet

buffet car
le wagon restaurant

porter
le porteur

luggage
les bagages

tunnel
le tunnel

ticket machine
le distributeur de billets

monorail
le monorail

signal box
la cabine d'aiguillage

smoke
la fumée

steam engine **la locomotive à vapeur**

going by water

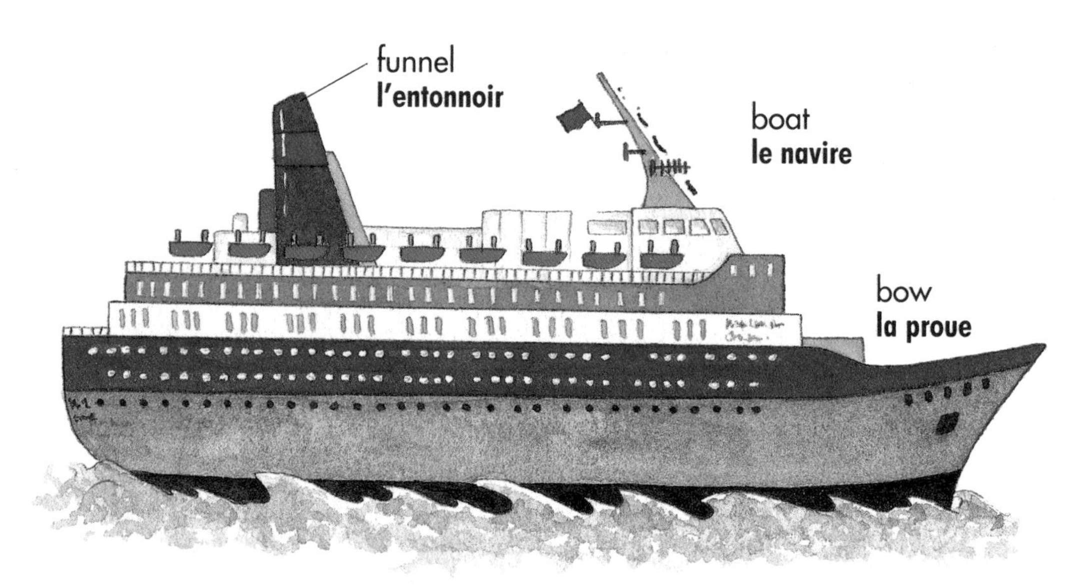

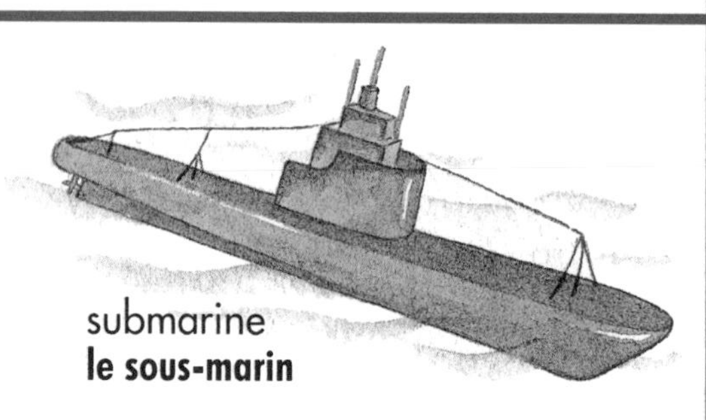

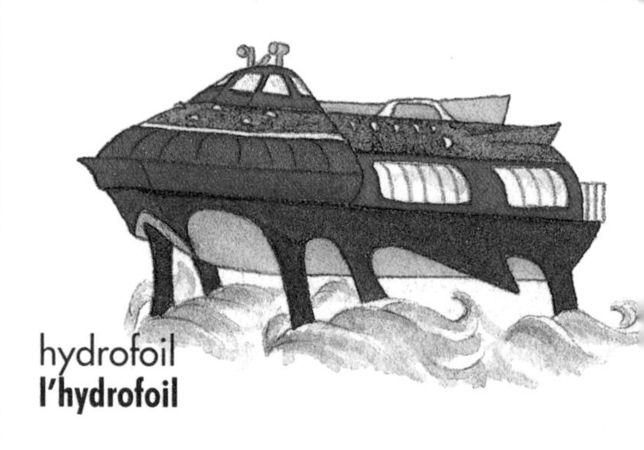

voyager sur l'eau

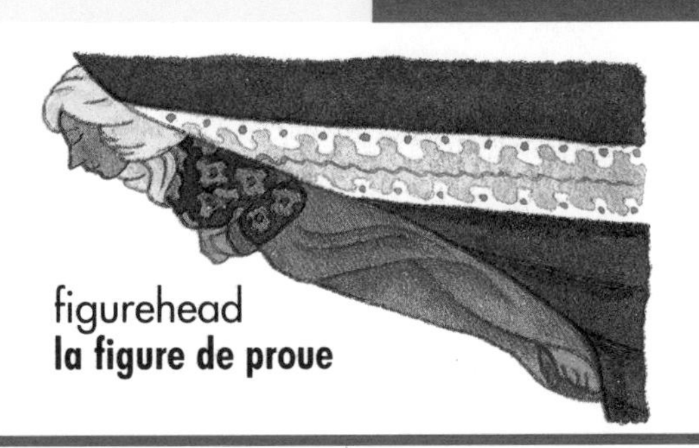

figurehead
la figure de proue

rowing boat
la barque

oar
la rame

barge
la péniche

hovercraft **l'aéroglisseur**

paddle-steamer
le bateau à aubes

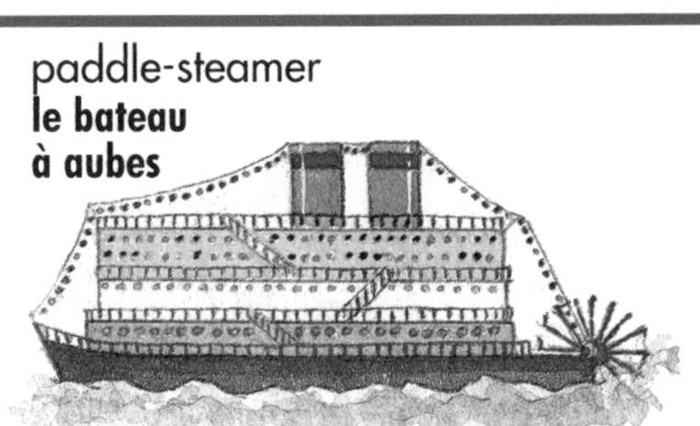

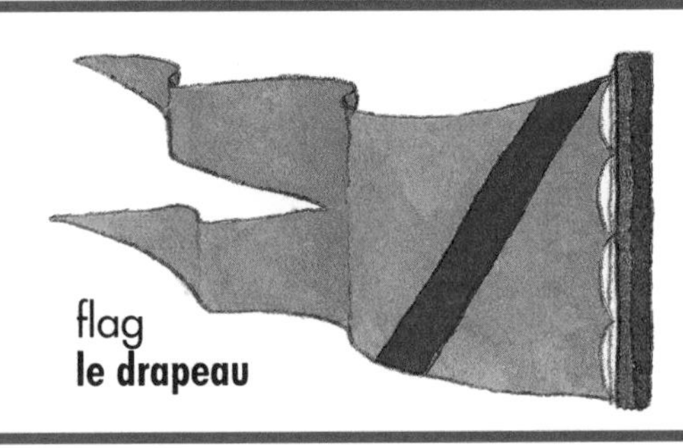

flag
le drapeau

speedboat
le hors-bord

ferry-boat
le ferry-boat

houseboat

la péniche aménagée

sails
les voiles

going by plane

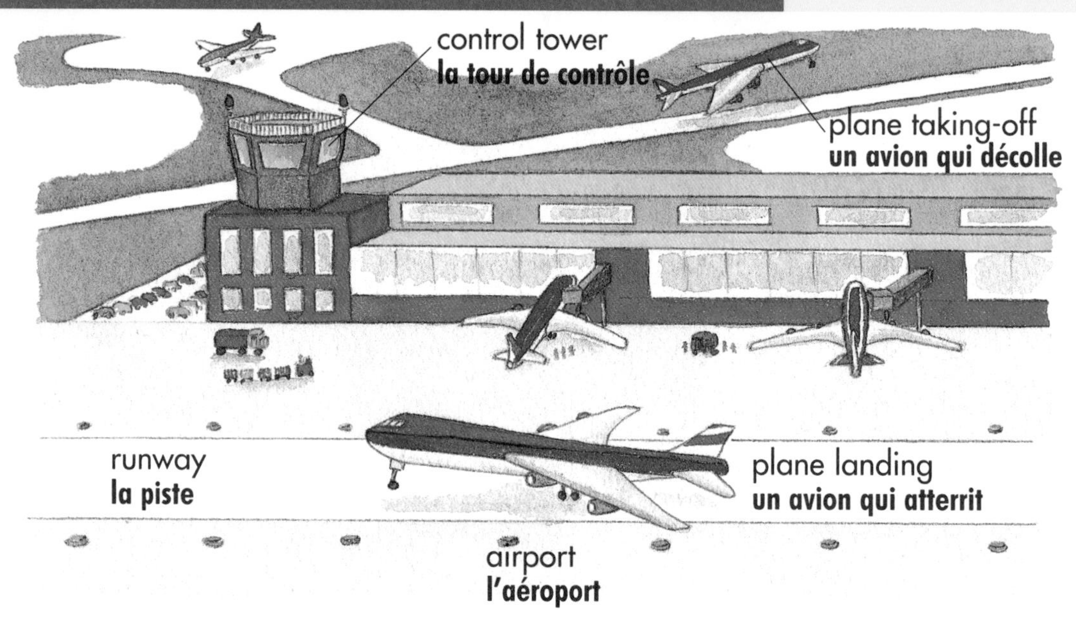

control tower
la tour de contrôle

plane taking-off
un avion qui décolle

runway
la piste

plane landing
un avion qui atterrit

airport
l'aéroport

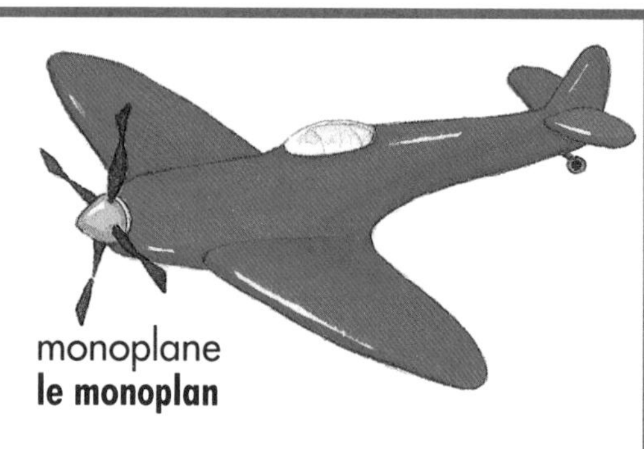

monoplane
le monoplan

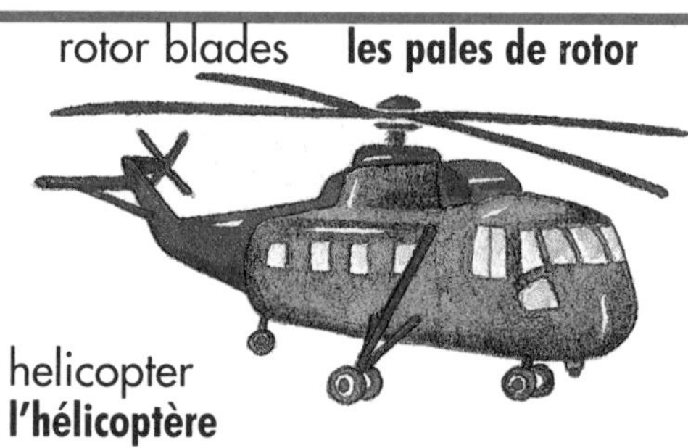

rotor blades **les pales de rotor**

helicopter
l'hélicoptère

biplane
le biplan

fuel tanker
le camion-citerne

triplane
le tréplan

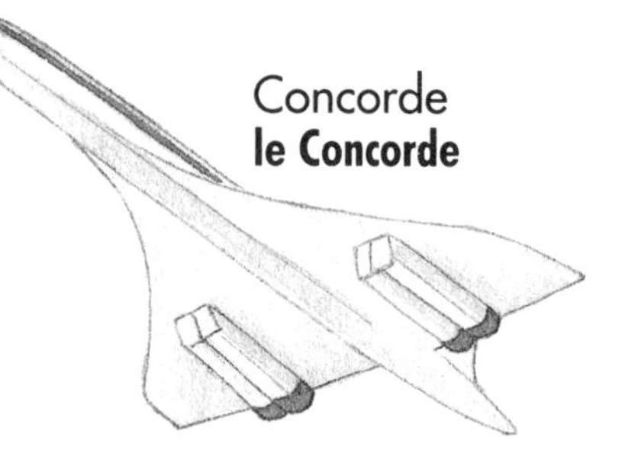

Concorde
le Concorde

air hostess
l'hôtesse de l'air

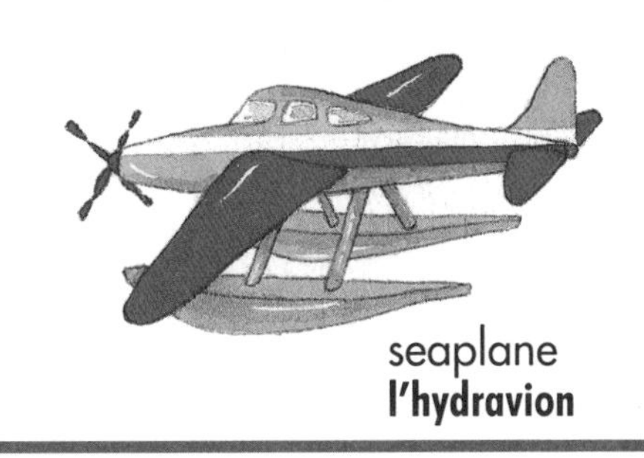
seaplane
l'hydravion

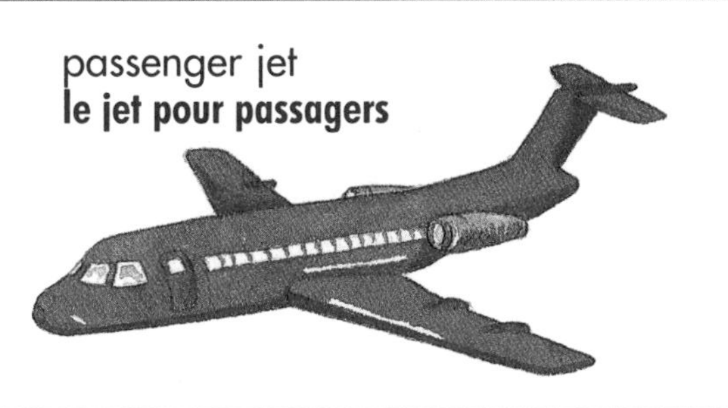
passenger jet
le jet pour passagers

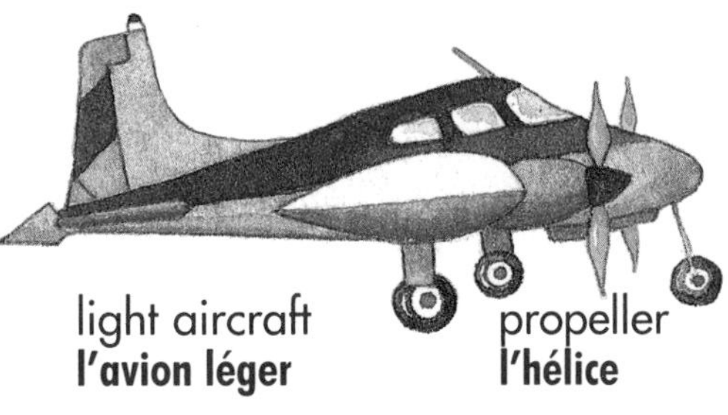
light aircraft
l'avion léger
propeller
l'hélice

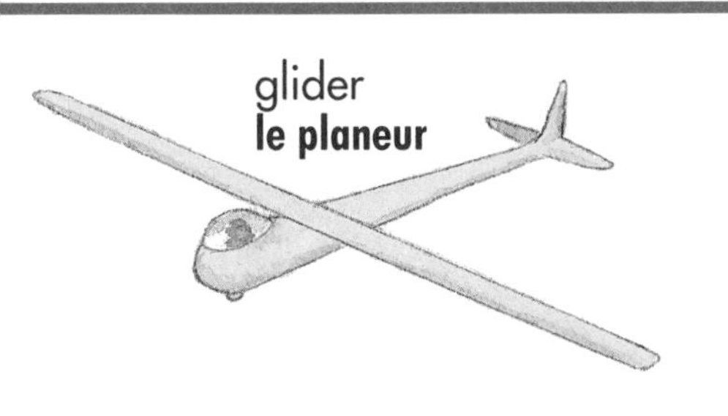
glider
le planeur

jumbo jet
le jumbo-jet

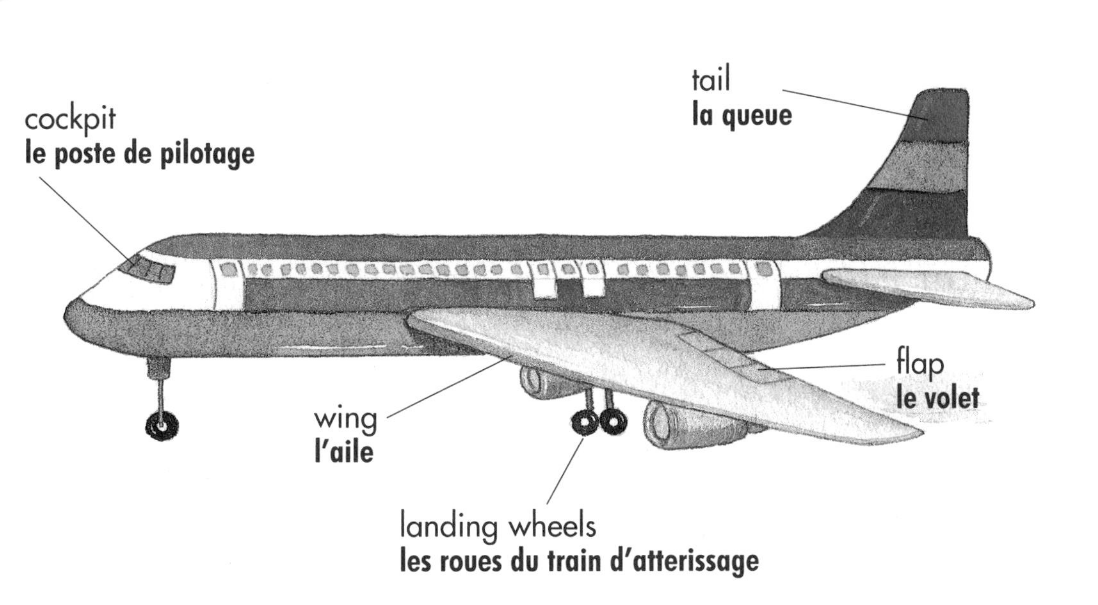
tail
la queue
cockpit
le poste de pilotage
flap
le volet
wing
l'aile
landing wheels
les roues du train d'atterissage

in the country

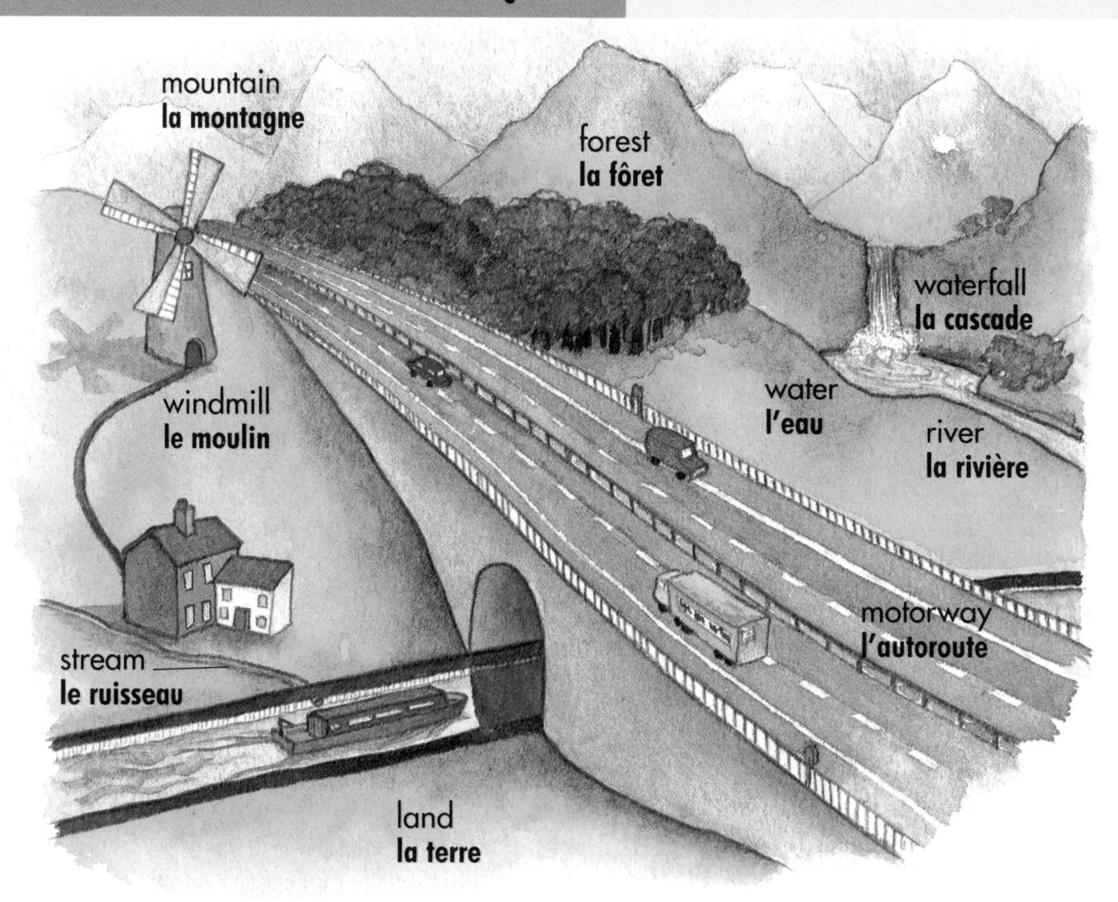

rocks
les rochers

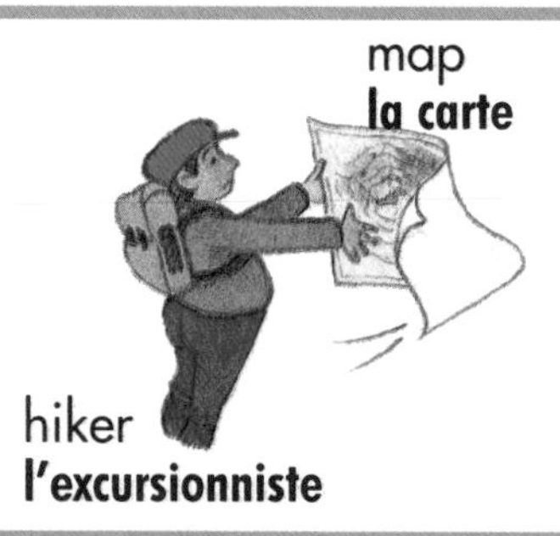

hiker
l'excursionniste

mobile home
la caravane

fishing rod
la canne à pêche

fishing net
le filet

fisherman
le pêcheur

trees
les arbres

scarecrow
l'épouvantail

wild flowers
les fleurs des champs

stepping stones
les pierres de gué

village
le village

town
la ville

city
la cité

builders and buildings

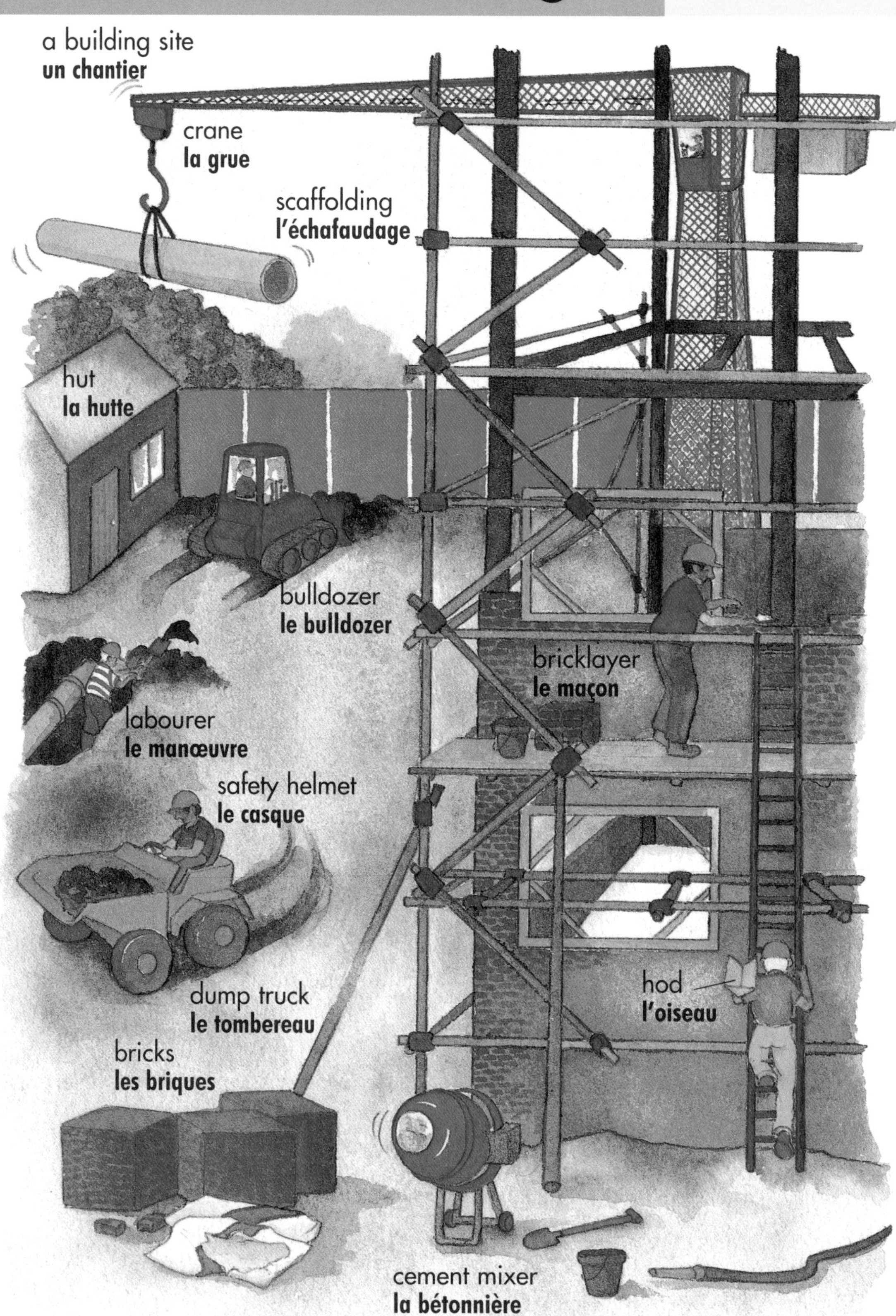

les entrepeneurs et les bâtiments

fire station
la caserne de pompiers

terraced houses
les maisons

cottage
le cottage

mosque
la mosquée

car park
le parking

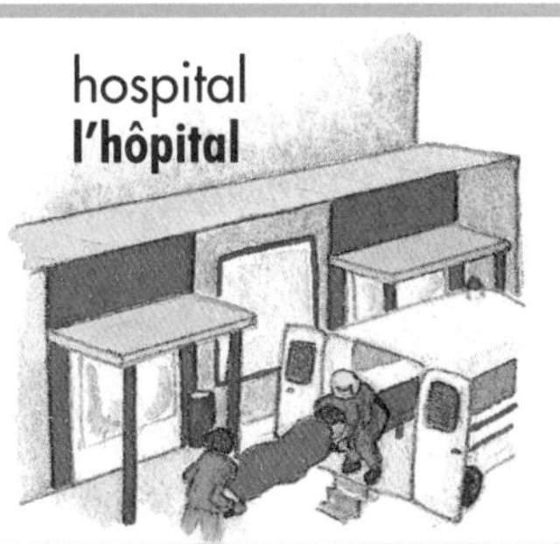
hospital
l'hôpital

art gallery
la galerie d'art

hangar
le hangar

castle **le château**

boathouse **le hangar à bateaux**

museum
le musée

tower
la tour

weather

le temps

winter
l'hiver

spring
le printemps

lightning
l'eclair

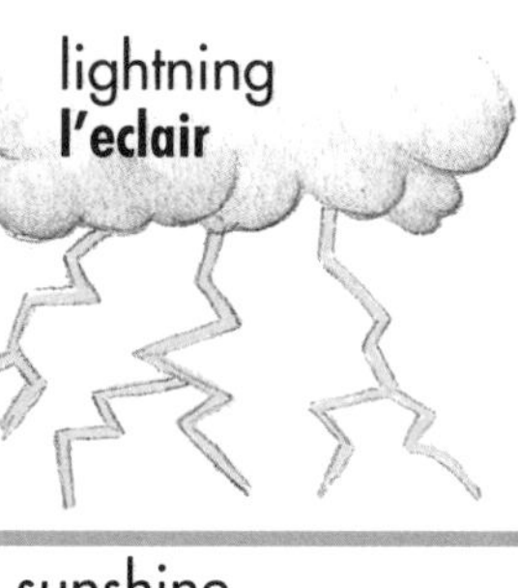

sunshine
la lumière du soleil

summer **l'été**

autumn
l'automne

rainbow
l'arc-en-ciel

rain
la pluie

storm
l'orage

hail
la grêle

ice
la glace

snow
la neige

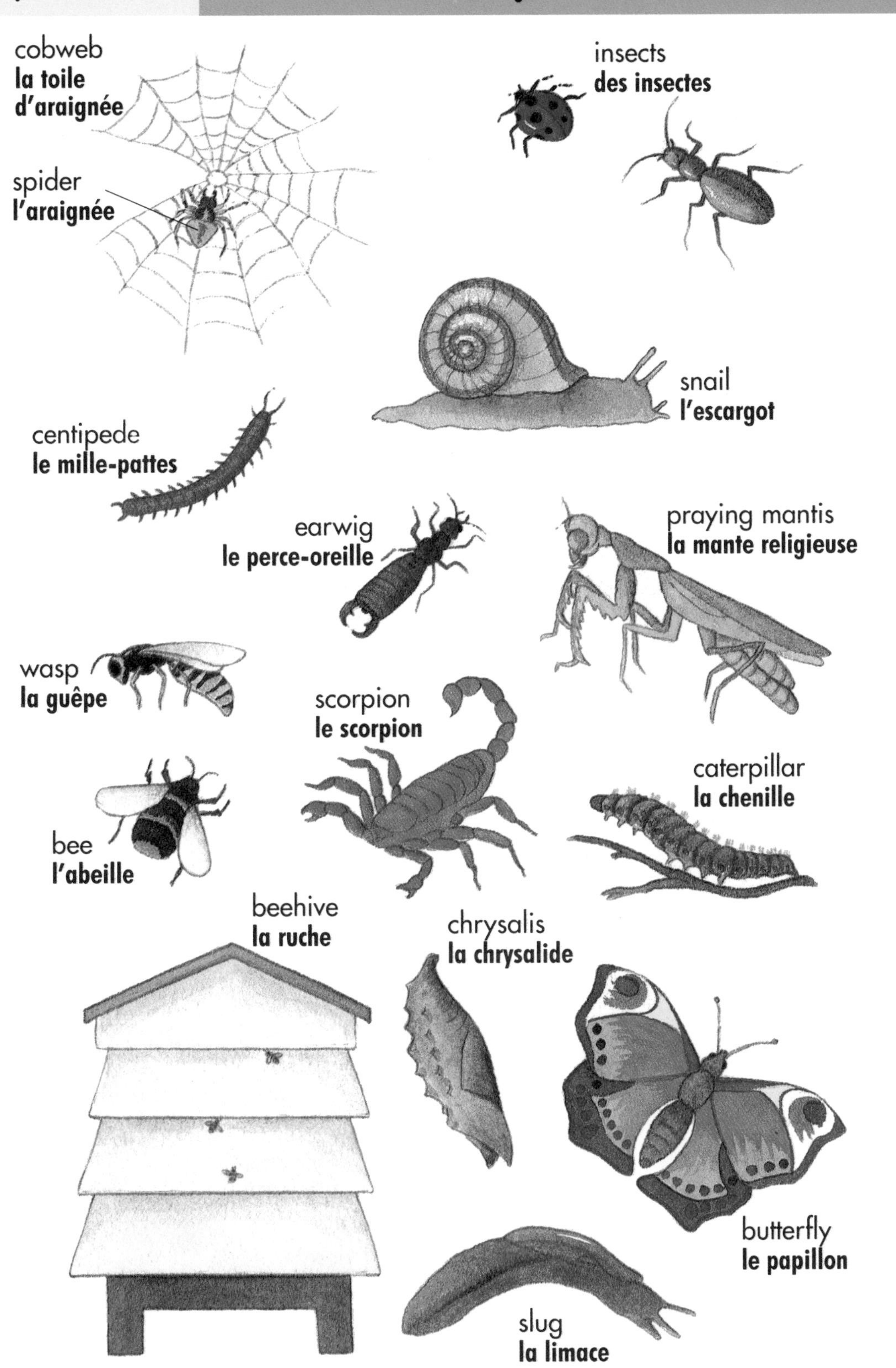
cobweb
la toile d'araignée
spider
l'araignée
insects
des insectes
snail
l'escargot
centipede
le mille-pattes
earwig
le perce-oreille
praying mantis
la mante religieuse
wasp
la guêpe
scorpion
le scorpion
caterpillar
la chenille
bee
l'abeille
beehive
la ruche
chrysalis
la chrysalide
butterfly
le papillon
slug
la limace

wild animals

penguin
le pingouin
woodpecker
le pic vert
stork
la cigogne
swan
le cygne
porcupine
le porc-épic
panda
le panda
crocodile
le crocodile
zebra
le zèbre
rhinoceros/rhino
le rhinocéros
hippopotamus/hippo
l'hippopotame
whale
la baleine

more wild animals

platypus
l'ornithorynque
armadillo
le tatou
seahorse
l'hippocampe
kangaroo
le kangourou
leopard
le léopard
koala
le koala
sloth
le paresseux
cobra
le cobra
boa constrictor
le boa constricteur
seal
le phoque
walrus
le morse

animal parts — des termes animaliers

les plantes plants

parts of a flower
les parties d'une fleur

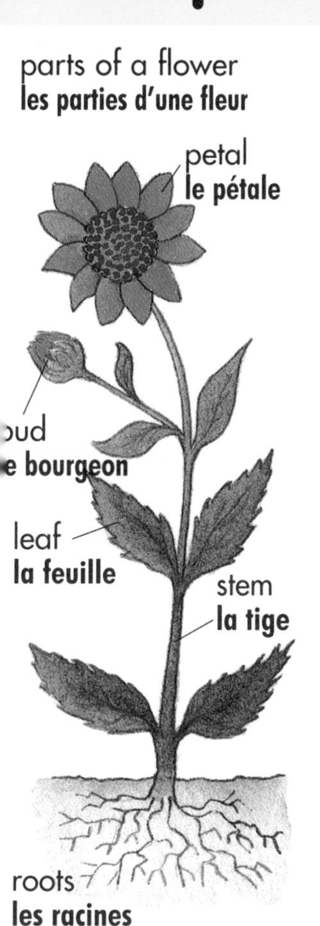

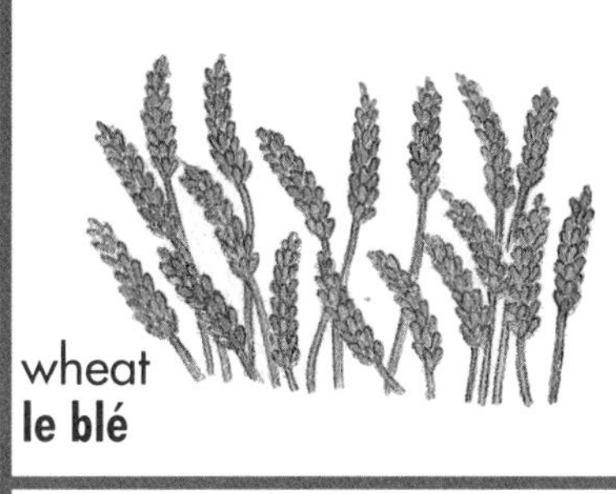

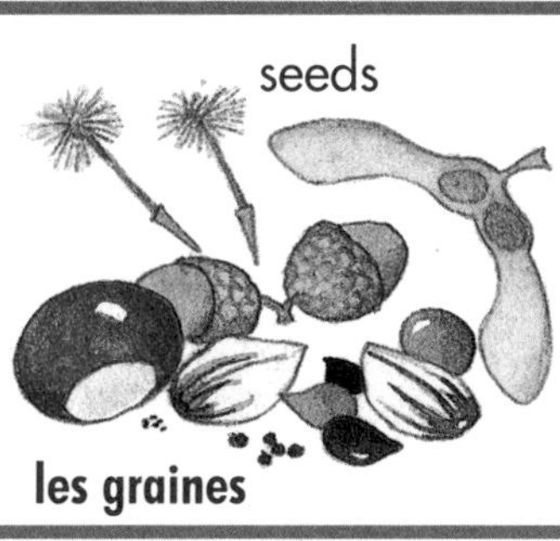

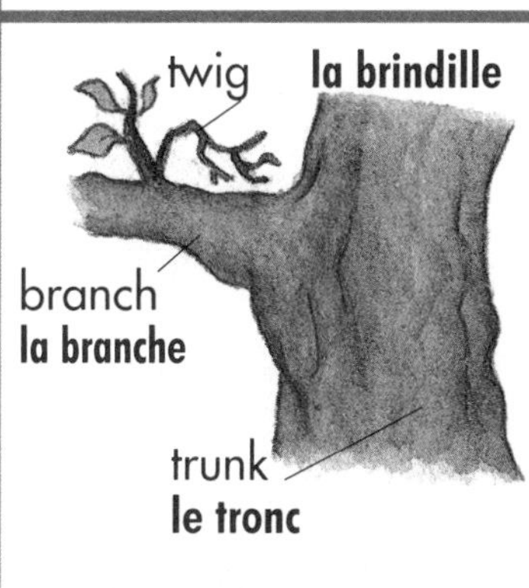

beside the sea

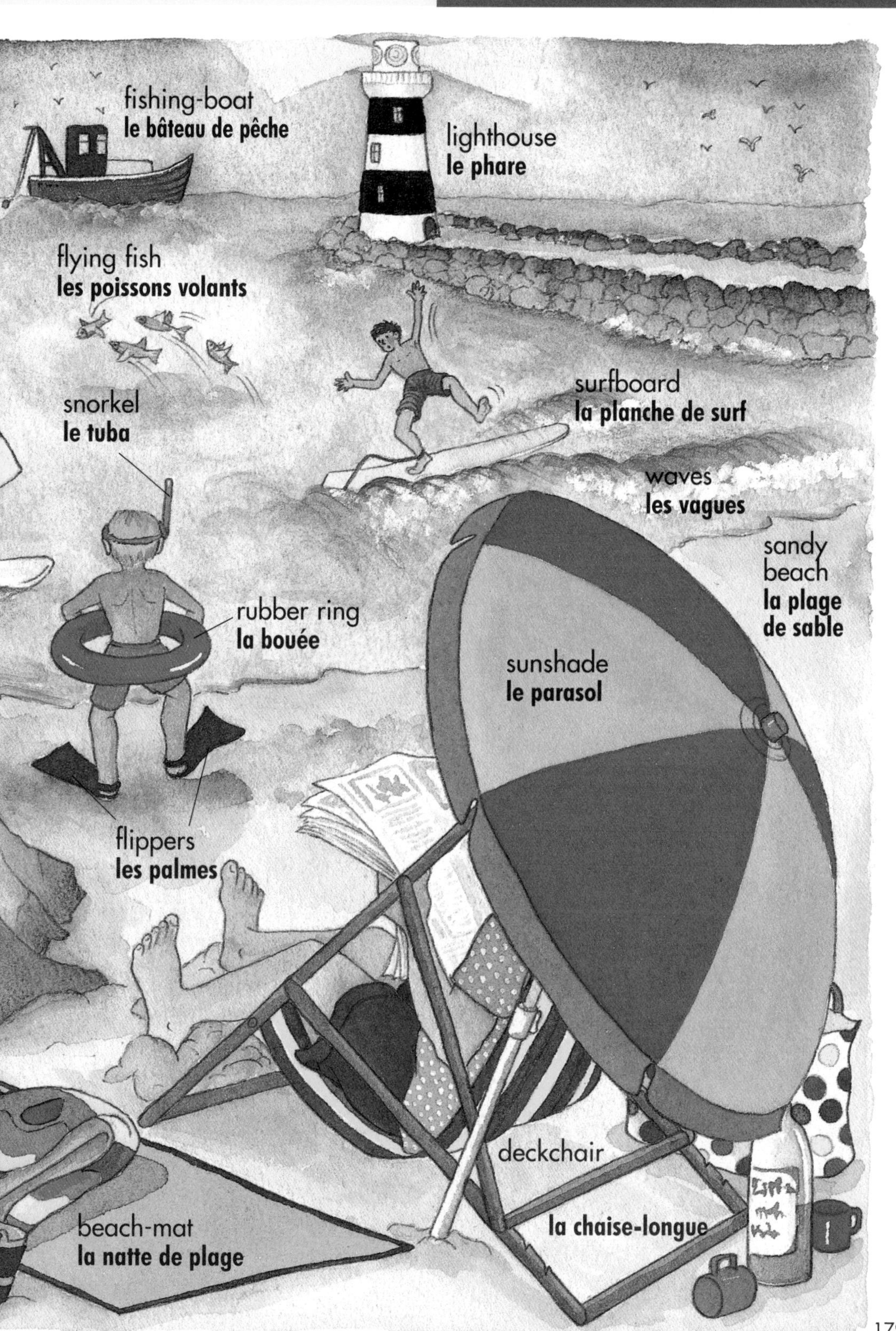
fishing-boat
le bâteau de pêche
lighthouse
le phare
flying fish
les poissons volants
surfboard
la planche de surf
snorkel
le tuba
waves
les vagues
sandy beach
la plage de sable
rubber ring
la bouée
sunshade
le parasol
flippers
les palmes
deckchair
la chaise-longue
beach-mat
la natte de plage

having a party

sparklers
les cierges magiques
magician
le magicien
party invitation
l'invitation
Please come to my fancy dress party
hostess
l'hôtesse
guest
l'invité
presents
les cadeaux
ribbon
le ruban
fancy dress costumes
les déguisements

opposites

over
par-dessus
under
sous
in
dedans
out
dehors
up
en haut
down
en bas
happy
heureuse
sad
triste
high
haut
low
bas
wet
mouillé
dry
sec

les contraires

storybook words mots de contes

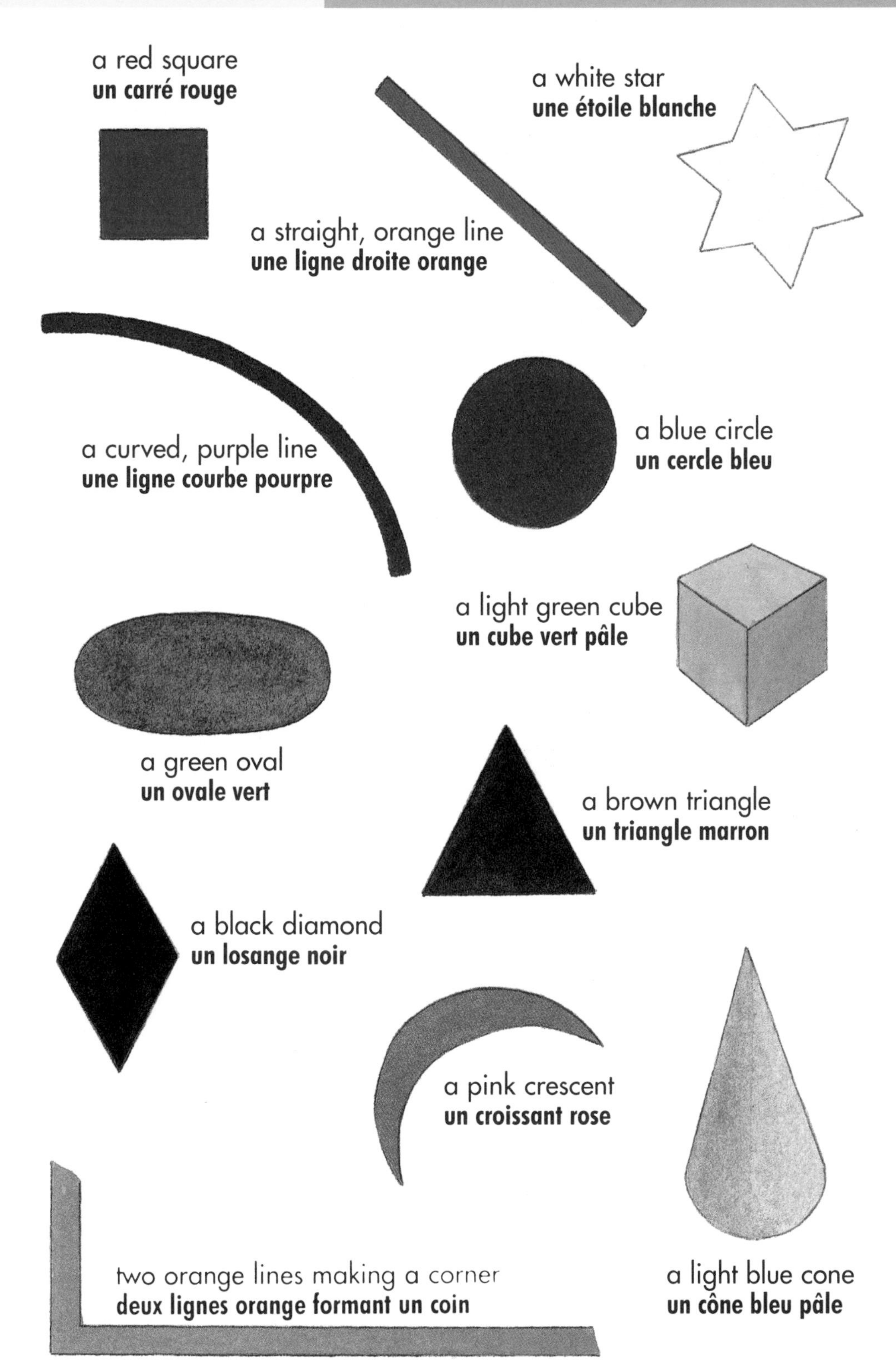
a red square
un carré rouge
a white star
une étoile blanche
a straight, orange line
une ligne droite orange
a curved, purple line
une ligne courbe pourpre
a blue circle
un cercle bleu
a light green cube
un cube vert pâle
a green oval
un ovale vert
a brown triangle
un triangle marron
a black diamond
un losange noir
a pink crescent
un croissant rose
two orange lines making a corner
deux lignes orange formant un coin
a light blue cone
un cône bleu pâle

numbers

1
one girl
une fille
2
two boys
deux garçons
3
three ponies
trois poneys
4
four cows
quatre vaches
5
five puppies
cinq chiots
6
six kittens
six chatons
7
seven lambs
sept agneaux
8
eight pigs
huit cochons
9
nine ducks
neuf canards
10
ten mice
dix souris

English words in this book/les mots anglais dans ce livre

ISBN : 0-7097-1428-9
This edition first published 2001 by Brown Watson
The Old Mill, 76 Fleckney Road,
Kibworth Beauchamp,
Leicestershire LE8 0HG, England

Reprinted 2002 (twice), 2003, 2005

Printed in Egypt